THE
SEEKING
YEARS

SIX TELEVISION PLAYS from the
award-winning CBS-TV Series

LOOK UP AND LIVE

edited by JOHN M. GUNN

Published for the
Cooperative Publication Association
by
THE BETHANY PRESS
ST. LOUIS, MISSOURI

812.5082
L 87 s
70 431
June, 1970

Distributed by Thomas C. Lothian, Melbourne, Australia, and Auck land, New Zealand and by the G. R. Welch Company, Toronto, Canada.

MANUFACTURED IN THE UNITED STATES OF AMERICA

CONTENTS

Introduction by Pamela Ilott 9

The Will to Win by Howard Rodman *rebel against death* 11 *29*

Plenty of Rein by Clair Roskam 31 *49*

The Puzzle by Clair Roskam 53 *71*

A Thing of Beauty by Howard Rodman 73 *p. 88*

No Man Is an Island by James Benjamin and Don Kellerman 91 - *106*

The Faith Hawker by Howard Rodman 109 *125+26*

General Production Notes 127

7

INTRODUCTION

Our Lord himself gave us the most striking precedent for the use of drama in religious education. The parables he used are so vivid that they spring to life in the mind's eye: the characters—housewives, shepherds, merchants, laborers—move across our vision with the animation of live actors; they are people we know in familiar situations.

Through the time-honored traditions of church re-enactments, of medieval moralities, and of passion plays, secular techniques have been used to teach religious truths. Radio and television were quick to utilize both the popularity and the persuasiveness of drama in their programing and the techniques and talent developed by professional broadcasters were available in no small measure to such organizations as the Broadcasting and Film Commission of the National Council of the Churches of Christ when they sought to develop the new tools in the service of God.

The Columbia Broadcasting System, for instance, inaugurating a religious program in the early days of television, drew on the same creative resources, experienced writers, and accomplished actors that were building the reputation of its outstanding dramatic shows. Through its Public Affairs Department, CBS developed a group of producers and writers who were not only specialists in the medium but who through such contacts as the B.F.C. were sensitive to the church's special needs and aims. Such writers are Howard Rodman and Clair Roskam, who are represented in this selection of scripts from *The Seeking Years.* This series of "Look Up And Live" programs was the successful fusion of their talent, the articulate concern of the church for young people today, voiced by John M. Gunn and Alva I. Cox, Jr., of the National Council of Churches, and the skills of an experienced CBS producer, Don Kellerman, and his staff.

9

The six plays published here consider many aspects of our common dilemma: On what do we base our standards?   What is ambition?   What is Faith?   How complex are the contending claims of our fellow men?   None seeks to give the ultimate answer, only to stir the imagination, only to invite exploration. Religious broadcasting is an accessory to, not a substitute for, the ministry.

These plays were designed for simplicity and did not rely on elaborate effects or complex settings to make their point.   It is all there, the power and the sensitivity and the passionate concern: to be read or to be restaged wherever there are people who care enough to speak aloud of the love of God and our fellow men.

> PAMELA ILOTT
> *Director of Religious*
> *Programing*
> *Columbia Broadcasting*
> *System*

THE WILL TO WIN

rebel against

By Howard Rodman

originally broadcast
June 2, 1957

The cast:

MARIAN_____Lyn Alstad

NICK_____James Bonnet

OWEN_____Clifford David

WOMAN_____Jacqueline Paige

PARABLE_____Jim Dimitri

JANITOR_____John O'Connor

COUNTERMAN_____Guy Raymond

NARRATOR_____Donald Symington

DIRECTED BY _____James MacAllen

SCENE

First, snow drifting down so slowly that all the world seems to be in slow motion. Beyond the snow, blackness. As the light comes up, we see a boy and a girl lying within a foot of each other: they are dressed in their mountain-climbing gear, and still linked together with the mountain-climber's rope. The boy holds the girl's hand as if he were still pulling her forward. The snow has partially drifted over them, and we get a sense of utter bleakness, with the wind whistling thinly in the background.

A newspaper headline is shown the audience: "Two Dead in Mountain Accident" and then the lights fade to a single spotlight on the NARRATOR, *who holds a snow-filled paperweight in his hands.*

NARRATOR: Despite what you see, they are not dead yet, though they may die in the end. But what you see is the result of a train of circumstances already in motion; and it leads, unless somewhere along the line it takes an alternative track, to death.

(He crosses through the blackness until he comes to the lighted area. This represents, in stylized setting, a college gym. There is a large gym window frame hung from nothing. For the rest there is a "horse," perhaps parallel bars, and a set of bar weights. In the foreground is a fencing mat on which two students, MARIAN *and* NICK, *are fencing.* OWEN *is lifting the weights in the background.)*

NARRATOR: Who I am—in case you're wondering—is unimportant. My function here is to serve as a catalyst for ideas and situations that confront all of us in some way—at some time.

(Turns to make introductions. As he approaches each one, the NARRATOR *introduces them without interfering with their activities. They are aware of him in the same*

13

way that the characters in "Our Town" are aware of the
NARRATOR.)

NARRATOR: This is Marian. And this is Nick. Marian is seventeen; she stands in the top third of her class. Nick lives for sports, and plans to make his career in teaching athletics in a college. He is in love with Marian. Marian is in love with Owen—(*Points*) That's Owen. (*He crosses to* OWEN) Owen is nineteen. He has only one goal: to be better than anyone else. Some men are natural athletes. Owen is a natural competitor; and though he lacks the easy coordination of Nick, for example, frequently, by his sheer determination to win, Owen can beat Nick.

(OWEN, *out of sheer will to conquer, finally lifts the weight. He sets it down and does it again, though in reality it is too much for him.*)

NARRATOR: To fill you in a little more, Marian is in love with Owen. Owen, so far as he is able, returns her love: meaning that he does not reject it. He uses it in many ways; always for himself. (*to* OWEN) Owen, will you leave that for awhile? Owen, why do you have to win?

OWEN: Because that's the way things are. There's no respect in this world for a man who doesn't win.

NARRATOR: Who taught you that?

OWEN: My father.

NARRATOR: Is that what he told you? That you must win?

OWEN: Told me? I never listened to any of his words. He taught me! Taught me! Look at him—
(OWEN *points. The lights fade to another area. A stylized set of steps, about three or four, and at the top, the door of a tenement house.* OWEN'S FATHER *stands there with a plumber's plunger on his shoulder, backing down the steps before the wrath of an angry* MATRON.)

MATRON: Don't tell me I stuffed the sink up! I didn't stuff any sink! I live here! I pay rent here! And that's what I pay rent for! For your services! Don't tell me I stuffed the sink. Just unstuff it! Unstuff it! And don't give me an argument, Mr. Janitor!
(*She goes back up the steps, through the door, slamming it.* OWEN'S FATHER *shakes his head as if to clear it.* OWEN *and the* NARRATOR *come into the scene.*)

OWEN: (*To the* NARRATOR) You see what I mean! (*Points to his* FATHER) He doesn't know how to win! Pop, I put you out of my mind a long time ago!

(OWEN'S FATHER *walks away, exits.* OWEN *turns to the* NARRATOR.)

Told me? He taught me!

(OWEN *walks away. The* NARRATOR *sits on the steps and talks directly to the audience.*)

NARRATOR: The world seems to be highly competitive. And the thing one learns is that the shape of the world determines the shape of a man's ideas, unless he is looking for truth and will not accept appearances. Who are the greatest race horses? The ones that win. Who are the greatest baseball players? The ones that win. Who are the greatest men? The ones who win a place for themselves; who win fame, reputation, and riches. This seems to be the shape of the world. And Owen accepts it as a fact. Therefore, to understand Owen you must understand this parable. Look! (*He points.*)

(*Another area of light. A dollar bill lies on the ground. From two different directions come two* MEN. *One* MAN *stoops, reaching for the bill. The other* MAN'S *foot comes down hard on the hand. The* MAN *that first reached for the bill stiffens with pain: he tries to hold the bill, but pain causes him to relinquish his grip. He withdraws his hand and backs off. Then the other* MAN *reaches down and takes the bill. The lights shift to reveal* OWEN *and the* NARRATOR *standing and watching the scene as the* MAN *who got the bill puts it into his pocket with satisfaction.*)

OWEN: There is a successful man.

NARRATOR: There is an immoral man!

OWEN: You stand by yourself in that opinion. The world agrees with me.

NARRATOR: You're a Christian, Owen. Is that what Christ taught?

OWEN: Who believes what Christ taught? Open your eyes. Don't listen to the words; watch what people do! The world honors the man who gets the prize!

(OWEN *walks away. The* NARRATOR *speaks directly to the audience.*)

NARRATOR: And so it seems. If you pick up the want ads in the daily newspapers, you will see that aggressiveness is regarded as a desirable quality. How many times have you heard a question asked as to the moral qualities of a successful man? We ask usually what he has achieved materially. But these things cannot be regarded as conclusive. We must search a little more deeply. We must see whether the appearance matches reality. *(Calls)* Will you play the parable again, please?

(The lights dissolve to the money lying on the floor. Once again, the two men come into the picture. Again we see the struggle. Behind them is OWEN, *and to one side of* OWEN *is* MARIAN. MARIAN, *too, is watching the scene. The* FIRST MAN *reaches for the bill. The* SECOND MAN *steps on his fingers. The* SECOND MAN *gets the bill.)*

OWEN: There is a successful man! *(He starts to walk away, but* MARIAN *seizes his arm.)*

MARIAN: That was awful! Like animals in the jungle!

OWEN: It is a jungle!

MARIAN: No; we've come beyond that. Once we come to know shame we've come beyond the animals! *(She turns to the* MAN *who has the bill)* Do you know what you've done!

(The MAN *stuffs the money into his pocket and goes away guiltily, not able to look* MARIAN *in the face. He slinks away.* MARIAN *turns to* OWEN *again.)*

Don't you see? He knows what he's done! Look, he can't face us!

OWEN: But he has what he went after.

*(OWEN *walks away again.* MARIAN *follows a moment later, hanging her head. The* NARRATOR *speaks directly to the audience again.)*

NARRATOR: A voice raised against savagery! Think! It's not the first time you've heard a voice raised against savagery and selfishness and brutality. So that the world is not quite the way Owen thinks it is; there is a flaw in Owen's picture of the world. How deep does it go? *(Calls)* Play the parable again, please!

(The money on the floor once again. Again the FIRST MAN *reaches for the bill, and the* SECOND MAN *steps on his hand. This time the* FIRST MAN *looks up, but does not*

relinquish the bill, and something in his look causes the SECOND MAN *to retreat and withdraw his foot. The* FIRST MAN *rises, the bill in his hand. He holds it out to the* SECOND MAN.)

FIRST MAN: (*Gently*) If you need it so badly.

(*The* SECOND MAN *is ashamed and tries to turn away, but the* FIRST MAN *takes his hand and stuffs the money into it, closes his fist around it and exits. The* MAN *holding the money turns away, so deeply shamed that he flings the money away and flees.*)

(*The* NARRATOR *moves upstage.*)

NARRATOR: This is the flaw in Owen's picture of the world. He sees what he will see. He takes examples of violence and turns away from the recognition that the doctrine of Christ is a living force in the world!

(*The lights come up revealing the* NARRATOR *back in the gym area where* OWEN *and* NICK *are now fencing.* MARIAN *is watching.*)

NICK: Touché.

(*They back off from each other for a moment and then* OWEN *springs to the attack again with redoubled fury, so that finally* NICK *is forced to give ground. The* NARRATOR *crosses to stand beside* MARIAN. *Fascinated, caught up in the duel, she watches, tense, excited.*)

NARRATOR: You like a winner?

MARIAN: (*Never taking her eyes from the duel*) Yes.

NARRATOR: You're in love with Owen.

MARIAN: Yes.

NARRATOR: Even if he loses?

MARIAN: Yes.

NARRATOR: Don't you judge him and find him lacking at times?

MARIAN: (*For the first time she looks directly at the* NARRATOR) You don't judge somebody you love.

NARRATOR: Don't you?

MARIAN: No.

NARRATOR: You mean they're free to do whatever they please?

MARIAN: How can you give half of love? How can you say, I will love if everything you do pleases me?

NARRATOR: Can you love evil?

MARIAN: I don't look for evil in someone I love.

NARRATOR: But if you found it there?

MARIAN: Then I would hope that if I loved fully, my love would dissolve the evil.

(*She turns quickly at* OWEN's *shout of exultation.* OWEN *lunges and stabs* NICK *so hard his rapier doubles against the padding* NICK *wears.*)

OWEN: (*Triumphant*) Now!

(NICK *is stunned for a moment. Finally*)

NICK: Wow!

OWEN: (*Recovers his poise*) I'm sorry; I just got carried away.

NICK: No, everything's all right. Boy, that was something. Phew!

OWEN: I got carried away. Come on. Treat's on me.

(OWEN *puts his arm around* MARIAN's *shoulder and around* NICK's *shoulder and the three go off together. The* NARRATOR *strolls slowly toward the parallel bars.*)

NARRATOR: All this that you have seen was in the past, and yet is a part of the present; just as water flows from a tiny spring to become, a thousand miles and a hundred days later, a part of a great river.

(*He pulls himself up onto the parallel bars, swings a moment, then swings himself into a side-saddle sitting position on one of the bars, facing the audience.*)

NARRATOR: I used to wonder what was the purpose of becoming skillful at gymnastics, and then I learned the exultation of using my body to the full, of matching myself against my own potential. No matter. Now we have to know, in order to follow our story, what Nick is like. (*Calls*) Nick.

(NICK *enters, crossing to stand near the parallel bars, where he can talk to the* NARRATOR.)

NICK: How's it going?

NARRATOR: Well, I got up here.

NICK: It's what I told you; you've got to catch the rhythm of it.

NARRATOR: (*Nods*) Nick, who knew Marian first? You or Owen?

NICK: I did.

NARRATOR: What do you think of Owen?

NICK: It's hard to say. I admire him a great deal.

NARRATOR: Why?

NICK: He's so sure of himself. I'd like to be like that. When he wants something, he wants it so much! I'd like to be like that.

NARRATOR: Do you admire yourself?

NICK: I'm all right.

NARRATOR: But you'd rather be like Owen?

NICK: I guess I would.

NARRATOR: Are you jealous because Marian is his girl now?

NICK: A little. But I couldn't expect much else to happen once she met him.

NARRATOR: Then you didn't fight for her?

NICK: No, what would be the use?

NARRATOR: You might have won.

NICK: I might. But then I have to consider what Marian wants, don't I?

NARRATOR: Why?

NICK: That's obvious, isn't it?

NARRATOR: Nothing is obvious.

NICK: Because if you love somebody, don't you want them to have what they want?

NARRATOR: Would you let a child you loved have another ice cream cone if you knew it would give him a bellyache?

NICK: Owen's not a bellyache.

NARRATOR: You're sure.

NICK: I told you; I'd like to be like him.

NARRATOR: Thank you, Nick.

NICK: I'll see you later.

(NICK *exits. The* NARRATOR *swings down from the bars.*)

NARRATOR: And what Nick feels and what he did is part of the past and part of the present, too. But what we're most concerned about is the future, isn't it? The death of two young people; the needless death, since there are alternatives. I will take you back to the precise moment when this train of events began.

(*The* NARRATOR *crosses through the dark to another lighted area, this one representing an ice cream parlor on the campus. Again it is stylized. A counter hangs on wires, and there are four stools. One of the men who was in the parable of the dollar bill is behind the counter. The* NARRATOR *goes up to him.*)

NARRATOR: Do you remember the sixteenth of March?

COUNTERMAN: Was that the day the sophomores and the freshmen had the water fight?

NARRATOR: No, that was the day before.

COUNTERMAN: Oh, yes: the day they decided to climb the mountain.

NARRATOR: Yes, that day. Do you remember what happened?

COUNTERMAN: (*Thinks. He takes each detail from his memory separately.*) A whole bunch of them came in here. I remember it was a nice day, not too hot, not too cold. I could see right away they were all excited about something.

NARRATOR: How did the subject of mountain climbing come up?

COUNTERMAN: Well, Nick was the one. He'd been thinking about the way they climbed Mount Everest, and he thought what a great idea to climb Old Rockhead. It's not Mount Everest, but it's seven thousand feet high.

NARRATOR: Was Owen here while this was going on?

COUNTERMAN: I got to think about that.

(*He closes his eyes to visualize it. As he mentions a name, that person takes his place on one of the stools.*)
There was Nick; Nick was here. And Marian. And Owen didn't come in till it was all setttled, I think that's the way it was. Yes, it was that way.

(OWEN *enters and* MARIAN *goes to him, excited.*)

MARIAN: We're going mountain climbing!
(*She takes him by the hand to lead him to the others*)
Come on, we're just making plans!

NICK: I got the great idea we can have our own Everest.

MARIAN: The three of us and Carol and Bob are going too. We'll take Easter vacation.

NICK: We'll hire a guide. We'll make out plans; we'll get maps.

OWEN: Count me out.

MARIAN: What?

OWEN: Not me.

NICK: Gee. That messes up the whole thing.

OWEN: That's the way it is.

MARIAN: Why, Owen? Why won't you?

OWEN: Because I won't. Listen, we have a date later, don't we? I'll see you later.

> (*He goes. Just as at the entrance of* OWEN *everyone came out of their stylized frozen positions into aliveness, so now, as he leaves, they become frozen again. All except the* COUNTERMAN *and the* NARRATOR. *The* NARRATOR *is standing to one side, and the* COUNTERMAN *comes to him.*)

COUNTERMAN: That's the way I remember it.

NARRATOR: What happened after Owen left?

COUNTERMAN: Well, first they were going to kill the whole idea, and then they decided to go through with it without him. That was Marian's idea. She thought if they went through with it Owen would come in later. Nick didn't stay long after Owen left. Then a couple of coeds came in to the next table and started a big discussion about Jimmy Dean. They said that . . .

NARRATOR: Thank you.

COUNTERMAN: That's all right.

> (*The lights fade to indicate a time interval and then rise to reveal the* NARRATOR *sitting at a table in the same ice cream parlor.*)

NARRATOR: This is late afternoon. In a little while Owen is going to join Marian here. This is one of the moments when the train of events may have taken a different course.

> (MARIAN *arrives and the* NARRATOR *rises. The* NARRATOR *speaks to her.*)

NARRATOR: Owen'll be here in a minute.

MARIAN: Why won't he go with us? Do you know?

NARRATOR: Yes, I know. Because I know Owen.

MARIAN: Do you think you know him better than I do?

NARRATOR: You wouldn't believe that, would you?

MARIAN: No.

NARRATOR: Be very careful.   Think carefully what you say to him, please.

MARIAN: You don't know Owen as I do.

(*The* NARRATOR *walks away, passing* OWEN *as he enters the scene.   They nod to each other in passing.*)

OWEN: Hi.

MARIAN: I want you to explain to me; now.   Before anything else.

OWEN: I didn't want to go with the others.

MARIAN: The others?

OWEN: Yes, the guide and all the others.   I'm going alone.

MARIAN: Why?   Why can't you come with us?

OWEN: I'm going by myself unless you want to come with me.

MARIAN: Why can't we all go together?

OWEN: Because I'm not made that way.   I go on my own.   No one is going to guide me to the top of anything.

MARIAN: You won't come with us because it wasn't your idea.

OWEN: No, not because it wasn't my idea.   Because I go alone.

MARIAN: Why?

OWEN: Because that's the way I am.   Because I have to.   I'm going to be the first one to the top of that mountain.   I'm going to stand up there and look down and watch the rest of you coming up after me.

MARIAN: Why?

OWEN: Because I have to win.   And the rest of you don't care that much.

MARIAN: What difference does it make?

OWEN: I don't like people looking down at me.   I don't like second place or second choice.   I want to be the first and the greatest.

MARIAN: Why is it so important?   Explain it to me: I want to understand!

OWEN: Because that's the challenge!   What else is there except to win?

MARIAN: But no one's challenging you!

OWEN: I'm challenging them!

MARIAN: You can't live that way.

OWEN: Why can't I? How do you think I've been living? How do you think I made the football team? Half a dozen players are sitting on the bench that play better than me. But they don't care the way I do.

MARIAN: But you're making everyone else feel bad; you killed the whole fun of it by not coming.

OWEN: I don't care. I have to do it my way. No matter what!

MARIAN: I won't let you go alone!

OWEN: I told you, you can come with me.

MARIAN: No!

OWEN: Then you're forcing me to go alone!

MARIAN: No, it's not me, you can't blame it on me!

OWEN: Then come with me—

MARIAN: I don't know. I don't know.

OWEN: Think about it.

(*The* NARRATOR *comes back. He looks at her with compassion, but she is not aware of him.*)

NARRATOR: That was one of the moments when it was possible not to arrive at death in the end. But Owen couldn't be dissuaded. Not that the challenge of the mountain is secondary to the challenge of forcing Marian to do what he wishes. The will to win—no matter what.

(*The* NARRATOR *walks away from the bench through the darkness to the gym area.* NICK *is sitting, miserable, on the "horse"; too miserable to work out. The* NARRATOR *crosses to him.*)

NARRATOR: Taking it easy?

NICK: I don't feel like working out today.

NARRATOR: Did Marian tell you she's going with Owen?

NICK: Yes.

NARRATOR: What did you say?

NICK: What could I say?

NARRATOR: Is Owen experienced at climbing?

NICK: No.

NARRATOR: Isn't it dangerous, then?

NICK: Of course it's dangerous! What do you want me to do?

NARRATOR: What do you want to do?

NICK: I don't want to do anything. I'll tell you something; if it was anybody else, I'd put my foot down. But if I say anything to her, she'll think I'm jealous!

NARRATOR: And that's the reason you can't say anything?

NICK: There's another reason. If Owen says he can do it, he can.

NARRATOR: You believe that?

NICK: Yes.

NARRATOR: You give him a blank check?

NICK: Yes.

NARRATOR: Why?

NICK: Because he does what he says he will.

NARRATOR: And he will never meet with an accident?

NICK: No!

NARRATOR: And he will never fail!

NICK: No! Nothing's going to stop him!

NARRATOR: You could!

NICK: Why should I?

(NICK *jumps down off the horse and walks away. The* NARRATOR *turns directly to the audience. He ticks off on his fingers.*)

NARRATOR: Marian couldn't stop Owen. Nick wouldn't. But there was still Owen himself and there were circumstances. Three days before the climb was to begin, Owen sprained his ankle. (*He points.*)

(*The lights fade to a park bench.* OWEN *is sitting there holding his ankle.* NICK *and* MARIAN *come running up.*)

OWEN: I sprained my ankle.

NICK: Bad?

OWEN: I don't know.

MARIAN: I'm glad.

OWEN: What do you mean, you're glad?

MARIAN: Because I didn't want to go. And now you can't.

OWEN: Who says I can't?

MARIAN: Owen—everything is against you. You know as well as we do that they're expecting a blizzard on Big Rock in a few days. But—no—that's not going to stop you. What's a little snow to a man who's never climbed in his life? What's a blizzard to a boy who doesn't need a professional guide on a 7,000 foot climb? And now you sit there—with a sprained ankle—you sit there and you tell us "you'll still make it anyway"—Owen, what's the matter with you? This thing is almost spooky. It's as though you're defying the fates. It's almost like defying God.

(OWEN *pulls himself up. He tries his weight on the injured foot. He almost faints, but doesn't.*)

OWEN: In three days I'll be walking on this. I've got three days and I'll be fine. And if you want to back out, go ahead. But I'm going to be standing up there on the top of that mountain three days from now!

MARIAN: Owen, don't talk like that. Let it go a week.

OWEN: Leave me alone, will you?

(*He hobbles away.* NICK *and* MARIAN *look after him.* NICK *nods.* MARIAN *and* NICK *go off after* OWEN. *The* NARRATOR *enters the area and turns to the audience.*)

NARRATOR: Marian couldn't stop him. Nick wouldn't and Owen didn't know how to stop himself. And he wanted to; he wanted to very badly.

(*He crosses through the dark to another bench where* OWEN *is sitting. He sits beside him.*)

NARRATOR: Going to call your own bluff? (OWEN *nods.*) Don't you have enough sense to quit?

OWEN: I don't know the word "quit."

NARRATOR: It's a good word.

OWEN: Maybe for you.

NARRATOR: Do you think anyone would blame you if you quit?

OWEN: No, they wouldn't blame me. Because they'd understand that; they'd understand stopping halfway; they'd understand softness and indecision, because that's part of their life. But if I did what they'd do, then all I'd be is just somebody like everybody else. No, a long time ago I gave up the idea of quitting when it got tough.

NARRATOR: What did you gain?

OWEN: Me. I gained the right to stand and look down at *them.*

NARRATOR: Is that a good reward?

OWEN: Sometimes it's a little lonely. Otherwise it's fine. That's the way it is.

NARRATOR: I see.

(*He rises and walks away from* OWEN. *As he leaves, the light on* OWEN *dims out, leaving behind the last impression of a lonely* OWEN *slowly massaging the hurt ankle, then they come up to reveal the* NARRATOR, *in an undefined area as before, with the snow-filled paperweight in his hand.*)

NARRATOR: And so the snow began—as small a matter in the cosmos of God, as is this snow in this paperweight to us. And yet important, for he sees the fall of the sparrow, too.

(*The lights come up revealing a stylized little hut on the mountain. The snow is falling.* NICK *is there alone; he is sleeping.*)

NARRATOR: This is the day when the tragedy may happen, and two young people die.

(*The* NARRATOR *taps* NICK's *shoulder and wakes him.* NICK *comes awake all at once, reaching out for* MARIAN.)

NICK: Marian? Marian! My God, she's gone with him!

(NICK *starts to run after her, but the* NARRATOR *stops him.*)

NARRATOR: Wait a minute, Nick. It may happen that way, but it hasn't happened yet. You haven't come up here yet, any of you!

NICK: I thought it was over. Then it's not too late!

NARRATOR: No, it's not too late this side of the mountain—the last refuge before the climb to the top. Owen and Marian will be along soon and you will be with them, Nick—Why?

NICK: Because he's going to come, and she's going to come with him. And if I can't save him, I'm going to save her.

NARRATOR: How?

NICK: I don't know. I'll talk to them; I'll do something. And if I can't do anything else, I'll go with them.

(*The lights dim to the* NARRATOR.)

NARRATOR: All right, Nick. Go back to sleep. You're dreaming.

(*The spotlight stays on the* NARRATOR *as he crosses to where* NICK *was. The space is now empty.*)

And so we come to the final possible crossroads. Nick knows what lies ahead and Marian, too. *(Calls)* Marian! Marian, see what's going to happen!

(The lights fade to the TWO PEOPLE *partially covered with snow. The following dialogue is delivered off-stage.)*

Do you see, Marian? This is the only way it can end.

MARIAN: And if I let him go himself, then he dies alone, doesn't he?

NARRATOR: Will he go by himself, Marian?

MARIAN: I don't know. I won't take the chance!

NARRATOR: Even though you know it ends in death?

MARIAN: What else can I do? I love him very much.

(The lights rise to reveal the hut again. The NARRATOR *is still there. He speaks directly to the audience.)*

NARRATOR: We'll wait here. They'll be along soon.

(OWEN *is the first to come, with* MARIAN *right after. Then a moment later comes* NICK. *It is snowing harder now, and the wind is strong and shrill and bleak.)*

MARIAN: I can't go any farther.

OWEN: Then wait here.

MARIAN: No, wait; I'll go with you. Just give me a minute to catch my breath.

OWEN: A minute. Because I haven't any time to lose.

(NICK *leans against the hut, panting.)*

NICK: We can't make it after this, Owen. You couldn't make it with a good leg. You can't take Marian up there with you.

OWEN: She's coming because she wants to. I'm not making her.

NICK: Listen, Owen, listen to reason!

OWEN: I don't want any part of your reasons!

(OWEN *rises to start off.)*

NICK: Owen, I can't make it. Stay here with me, will you?

MARIAN: You wait here, Nick. We'll be back.

NICK: Marian, don't go with him, please!

MARIAN: I have to, Nick. I can't leave him alone!

NICK: Okay. Then I'm coming with you.

(He grabs OWEN's *arm and swings him around.)*

I just want to say something to you. No matter what you say, you're dragging us after you, because you're too selfish to let us off the hook. Okay, go ahead, and we'll come with you, because maybe we're soft and maybe because I don't know how, and Marian doesn't know how to let a man go to his death alone. Go ahead. We're behind you.

(He clips his rope to MARIAN's *belt and* MARIAN *starts to clip her rope to* OWEN's. *And then she stops.)*

MARIAN: No.

OWEN: What do you mean, no! You're not going to quit now!

MARIAN: I am!

OWEN: How can you quit now? There's the top! You can almost see the top!

MARIAN: No, I can't, Owen. I can't let you drag both of us after you. Maybe you don't care about yourself; that's not all right but there's nothing I can do about it. And if you don't really care about me, that's not all right, but I love you so much I would have to go with you. But you're dragging Nick, too. Because you don't care about anything except yourself.

OWEN: I've got to get to the top, Marian. Don't you understand?

MARIAN: Then go alone! Because there's only room at the top for one anyway; your top.

*(*OWEN *nods.* NICK *puts his arms around* MARIAN *to comfort her.* OWEN *looks at them, then goes, and disappears in a moment.)*

NICK: You wait here, I'll go with him.

MARIAN: No. Because if either of us goes, there's nothing to stop him. I didn't see before, but when you don't judge, even someone you love, then you don't give them anything to help change them. Nobody can have a blank check, nobody.

(They sit down and wait, and the snow falls. They are so tired they can hardly keep their eyes open. They strain to stay awake, but finally they fall asleep. Then, through the snow comes OWEN, *staggering, exhausted. He comes and faces the* NARRATOR.)*

NARRATOR: Did you make it to the top?

OWEN: No, I turned back.

*(*OWEN *stumbles on his bad foot around the corner of the hut. As he enters* MARIAN *and* NICK *awaken.)*

MARIAN: Owen—are you all right?

OWEN: It was—it was too lonely up there. Even for me.
(He drops to his knees beside MARIAN *and embraces her.* NICK *grins, and shrugs. He punches* OWEN *in the shoulder and rises to leave* OWEN *and* MARIAN *alone. The lights dissolve and rise on the* NARRATOR, *again carrying the paperweight snowstorm. He speaks to the audience.)*

NARRATOR: And so, in the end, a happy ending. And I must say I believed it would be happy, all along I believed that. For I believe in the humanity of human beings. How could I do otherwise? If I couldn't see what might be good in the worst man, knowing that man is God's creation; how could I then, not believing in man, have faith in God?

Curtain

PRODUCTION NOTES

Mood In adapting this play to the stage, bear in mind that the cabin set and its general area symbolically represent a place of tragedy, disaster, death. The blocking should be done with this fact in mind, so that when one wishes to feel life, to rebel against death, he steps *away* from this area in one direction, toward life.

Sets There are five areas needed in the pattern suggested below:

1. Downstage left a small table with three chairs—the ice cream parlor.
2. Upstage from this the gym area, with a "horse," parallel bars, a fencing strip, and bar bells. (If the heavier pieces of equipment are not available, the suggestion of a gym can be carried out by hanging flying rings, or as simple a prop as a tumbling mat.)
3. Upstage center a step unit of three or four steps. The "lost dollar" parables may be played before this unit.
4. Downstage right is the cabin set, consisting of a cot and threefold flats. If flats are not available, a threefold screen will suffice, but only if it is large enough to give the actors room to move around in the area. The set should give a cramped feeling, but never one in which the actor is restricted.
5. Downstage center a limbo unit, for the narrator.

Exits There should be three exits at least, one directly behind the step unit. An escape unit is suggested, or some other means whereby the players may leave the set from the steps. The other two exits may be downstage left and right.

Costumes For the boys in the gym set, sweat pants and shirt; for Marian, shorts. In the mountain scene, the actors can wear ski clothes, or in general any rough winter clothing. Climbing gear, if available, will add to the effect.

Miscellaneous To replace the newspaper headline—the device of a newsboy. Enter SR, crosses stage with line: "Extra. Read all about it. Extra. Two dead in mountain climb. Extra."

PLENTY OF REIN

By Clair Roskam

originally broadcast
June 9, 1957

The cast:

WENDY _____.Pamela King

EDNA _____Ruth White

RICHARD_____ Warren Berlinger

KEITH_____George Mitchell

NARRATOR_____.Donald Symington

DIRECTED BY _____James MacAllen

SCENE

As the curtain rises, we see spotlighted a young man—late twenties or no more than thirty. This is the NARRATOR.

NARRATOR: Imagine with me for a while—a man of about forty.
   (The lights go up on a man of that age over the NARRATOR's *shoulder and some distance behind him.)*
NARRATOR: And give him a wife.
   (Lights go up on a woman over his other shoulder.)
NARRATOR: And say they're typical middle class. General run. Ordinary as we can make them. And say they're parents. And then ask them something like this:
   (He turns his back to the audience to speak to the man and woman.)
Every man needs freedom to come into his own. How much freedom do you give your son? How much do you give your daughter?
MAN: A lot more than I had at their age.
WOMAN: We're liberal with our children.
MAN: We trust them.
WOMAN: We give them all the freedom of their contemporaries.
MAN: We give them all the freedom in the world.
   (The NARRATOR *turns to the audience again.)*
NARRATOR: These people are good people, like most people. But it could be . . .
   (Suddenly, the circles of light which have enclosed the MAN *and* WOMAN *grow larger, revealing that each holds a pair of leather straps. As we watch, the straps grow taut and are jerked back, bringing onstage a* BOY *and a* GIRL. *The* BOY, *nearly eighteen, is attached by one rein to his father and by the other to his mother, as is the* GIRL, *seventeen.)*

NARRATOR: . . . that they're lying.

(The lights go out on the four people and come up almost immediately on a structure of lathes that suggests the frame of a house. There is an area defined as a living room by an easy chair, a sofa, and a lamp. There is also a telephone. A kitchen area is similarly defined by a counter and a breakfast table. There is a railing, about three feet high, which encloses the house. During the blackout, the actors have taken their places, and now we see that the MAN sits in the easy chair and disappears behind a newspaper. The WOMAN moves to the kitchen and works among the pots and groceries on the counter. The BOY and the GIRL take places at the railing and look dreamily out. The NARRATOR speaks over the pantomime to the audience.)

NARRATOR: I'm a student. Graduate school. Philosophy. When I've got my degree I'll teach, I imagine. Though a philosopher's job is not so much teaching as learning, and learning not so much the answers as what the questions are—very often they're not easy to find. What are the real questions facing the people I'll stand before? Do they know? Can I help find them? Sometimes I dream up whole families just to test myself. Like this one here. I call these the Williamses. This is Edna.

(The WOMAN acknowledges the audience.)

EDNA: How do you do.

NARRATOR: And Keith.

(The MAN does not move from behind his paper.)

EDNA: Keith!

KEITH: *(Surprised)* Oh—pleased to meet you.

NARRATOR: Wendy.

WENDY: Hello.

NARRATOR: And Richard.

RICHARD: Hi.

NARRATOR: The Williamses are a nice family. Good, prosperous, happy-looking people—what questions do they face, about Wendy and Richard, for instance, on the verge of their adult life? An ancient philosopher remarked of youthful character:

"All their mistakes are in the direction of doing things excessively." What questions does this raise for parents? How much rein do they give the excessiveness of youth?

EDNA: Our kids get plenty of rein.

NARRATOR: I see.

EDNA: We trust them completely.

KEITH: And for that matter you'll find kids are pretty conservative if you leave them on their own.

EDNA: There's a lot of talk about delinquency, but after all, that is the exception.

NARRATOR: What you're saying is that Wendy and Richard are well behaved.

EDNA: Perfectly.

KEITH: Reasonably.

EDNA: Well, yes, Keith is right. If you ask me if I approve of everything they do a hundred per cent, well, of course not.

KEITH: Richard is a good boy, but he's not as responsible as he ought to be.

EDNA: Things are different, Keith, than when you were a boy. He isn't called upon to be so serious and responsible as you were.

KEITH: That should make it simpler.

EDNA: Maybe so. I'll trust Richard when the chips are down.

KEITH: Well, so would I. He's a sound boy. Now, I don't mean anything different . . .

EDNA: It's Wendy that worries me just a little. She's a bright girl—but she's frivolous.

KEITH: She tends to her business.

EDNA: Barely. It'd be nice sometime to see her really apply herself to her schoolwork, and once—just once—offer to lift her hand around the house.

KEITH: She's going to come out all right.

EDNA: Nobody said she wasn't going to come out all right.

KEITH: (*To the* NARRATOR) I think you better dream yourself up another family than the Williamses. We haven't got any serious problems. Our kids are okay.

NARRATOR: No difference of opinion?

KEITH: Between Edna and me? Oh, sure, but we talk those out.

NARRATOR: No, I mean with Wendy and Richard.

KEITH: *(Puzzled)* Difference of opinion? *(He looks to his wife.)*

EDNA: I don't know what you mean.

NARRATOR: They don't have opinions?

EDNA: Well, of course they do, but they're sensible youngsters —oh, I know, Keith. He means like the time we had the fuss with Wendy about hours, you know, and with Richard over the car.

KEITH: Oh, that kind of thing—

EDNA: We get through those all right. It was a few weeks ago. Wendy had a date— Oh, let me show you—

WENDY: *(She has moved into the kitchen and started to string beans)* I'm going to be late tonight, Mother.

EDNA: Ummm. We're going to have those beans tonight, dear. So hurry up a little, please.

WENDY: Don't wait for me, will you?

EDNA: I'm not usually in bed before eleven.

WENDY: Well, I won't be in by then.

EDNA: Why not?

WENDY: It's Friday, Mother. The dance won't be over 'til one and afterwards we'll all go out for a snack.

EDNA: And at about what time can we expect to see you back here?

WENDY: Oh, two o'clock, I suppose.

EDNA: Not on your life.

WENDY: Mother, I am seventeen years old—

EDNA: I don't care if you're a hundred and seventeen.

WENDY: Which just goes to show how unreasonable you are.

EDNA: That may be, Wendy. But you're not staying out 'til all hours of the morning. And that's that.

WENDY: You never cared if I stay up studying 'til one o'clock in the morning.

EDNA: I don't like it one bit.

WENDY: It's just going to embarrass me to death to have to run away from the dance before anyone else, like a little girl.

EDNA: Well, I'm sorry.

WENDY: I'd rather not go at all. In fact, I'm not going to go.

EDNA: *(Moving into the living room)* Keith, would you tell me, please, what you think of the idea of your daughter staying out 'til two o'clock in the morning?

KEITH: And you tell me what you think of Richard going away in the car for a whole week end.

RICHARD: You said yourself you're not going to use the car.

KEITH: That's not the point.

RICHARD: Look, Dad, I am eighteen years old.

KEITH: Not yet.

RICHARD: Almost.

EDNA: Where do you want to go?

RICHARD: Fishing.

EDNA: Well, I don't like that, Richard. If anything happens—

RICHARD: Nothing's going to happen.

EDNA: Listen, things are happening all the time.

RICHARD: Just every once in a while I'd like it if someone would show a little confidence in me around here.

KEITH: We've got plenty of confidence in you, Rich. But after all, you're asking a lot. A seventeen-year-old boy—

RICHARD: Eighteen.

KEITH: —running off for the whole week end with the family car.

WENDY: I would like to know, please, if I can keep my date for tonight, or if I have to call it off.

KEITH: What are you asking for?

EDNA: She wants to know if she can stay out until two o'clock in the morning.

KEITH: Well, she can't.

EDNA: Well, that should make it final.

WENDY: Every girl in my crowd is going to stay to the end of the dance, and then go and get something to eat.

EDNA: If Betsy Norris is, I should be very much surprised.

WENDY: Well, she is.

EDNA: Mrs. Norris is a very good mother.

WENDY: Call her and ask her.

EDNA: I don't have to call her. I know very well—

WENDY: Call her and ask. (EDNA *studies her daughter for a moment, turns to the phone and dials.*)

RICHARD: Dad, please, will you just keep cool for a minute and listen to me?

KEITH: Richard, it's a rare day when I don't let you have that car if it's free and you want it.

RICHARD: I know it is.

KEITH: But there is such a thing as pushing a good thing too far.

RICHARD: If you had any confidence in me at all—

EDNA: Mrs. Norris? This is Edna Williams. How are you?

KEITH: Look, Son, to take it a hundred miles out of town for a whole week end—

RICHARD: There's no way of getting there except with a car.

EDNA: Well, we're just about to eat, too. Wendy's getting ready to go to the dance. I don't like the idea of them staying out so late. I suppose Betsy's going to go, too?

RICHARD: Chester Nelson's got his folks' car three times in a row. You want me to be a parasite?

KEITH: You mean to tell me Nelson lets that boy take his car out of town for a week end?

RICHARD: How do you think we get up there?

KEITH: Well.

WENDY: Well, ask her, Mother!

EDNA: Wendy seems to think the whole crowd is going to stay 'til the end of the dance. But I think that's kind of late, don't you?

RICHARD: If I had a car of my own, you wouldn't think anything about it. Lot of guys got cars of their own.

KEITH: We've got to talk this over with your mother, Richard.

EDNA: Ummmmmm-hmmmmm. Yes. Well, I suppose once in a blue moon— All right, then. I just wanted to know how you felt about it. We'll be talking soon, Mrs. Norris. (*Hangs up.*)

WENDY: Well. Now what do you say?

EDNA: Look, Keith, if all the girls are going to be staying out—

KEITH: That late?

EDNA: If Betsy and Julie and all the rest are going to be out, we don't want to look like cranks, do we?

KEITH: This isn't a precedent, young lady, and you remember that.

WENDY: Well, of course, I will. *(She kisses her mother and hurries out of the room.)*

KEITH: I don't like that.

EDNA: Well, neither do I.

RICHARD: I'd like to get the word about the car.

EDNA: I thought you did.

KEITH: A lot of boys Richard's age have cars of their own, Mother.

EDNA: Yes, and someday Richard will, too.

KEITH: If Nelson let Chet drive them up there half a dozen times—

EDNA: Keith, I'll be worried sick.

KEITH: Well, I think you're kind of going overboard, Mother.

RICHARD: And I'm a good driver. You said that yourself. Didn't you? Didn't you?

EDNA: It's your car, Keith. (KEITH *hands him the keys.)*

RICHARD: Thanks! Thanks, Dad. *(He hurries off.* EDNA *and* KEITH *turn now to the* NARRATOR *who has been standing inconspicuously watching the whole proceedings.)*

EDNA: Now, I think you can see that when there is a difference of opinion, we give our children a great deal of independence. We're very permissive.

KEITH: We're probably too permissive, in fact.

EDNA: Oh, I don't know, Keith. As you said yourself, we know we can trust them.

KEITH: Well, sure we can trust them.

EDNA: They're very good children.

KEITH: But I suppose I have to face it, I'm a little stuffy. When I was Richard's age I didn't have the money and the car and the freedom to move around that he has. Not by a long shot. I had to get out and work for it. I don't begrudge him that, but it just does seem a little premature.

EDNA: It doesn't seem so long ago to me that I was Wendy's age. And I remember a lot of talk about the looseness of the younger generation. Grandma used to let on to the aunts that I was kind of "fast." But I don't think that I turned out too wild and woolly, have I, Keith? But if I'd asked for the liberty or the privileges Wendy does, or kept her hours—ho ho!

KEITH: We don't try to make our children live our childhood over, and that's all there is to that.

EDNA: We give them freedom because people their age have freedom these days. And because we know they're sound at heart. And that, I think, answers your question.

NARRATOR: I wonder whether it does.

(EDNA *and* KEITH *freeze in position. The lights dim on the "house" area, and a light picks up* RICHARD *who enters from one side of the stage.*)

RICHARD: It doesn't.

NARRATOR: Why not?

RICHARD: It's not much of a test, that's all. I'm old enough to drive—old enough to make decisions for myself. But who did Dad listen to? Was it me? It was not. It was Mr. Nelson. I had to make use of another guy's father to get something I wanted. It was a matter of public opinion—not personal trust in me.

(WENDY *is similarly illuminated in a different position*)

WENDY: And was it any different with me? I looked at my mother and knew that if I were going to go to that dance it would only be because everyone else was going. Mother likes Mrs. Norris—admires her. But what about me? Does she trust me? I don't know. I've never known. My decisions have never been my own. Don't parents realize they can't play God?

(RICHARD *and* WENDY *disappear as the lights dim up again on the "house" area and the actors unfreeze.*)

NARRATOR: (*To* EDNA *and* KEITH) Do you play God?

EDNA: That's ridiculous, young man. We try to be decent parents and that's not playing God. Just wait 'til you have a girl Wendy's age out late at night and see how easy you find it.

KEITH: Or a boy with a car on the road for a whole week end.

NARRATOR: I don't mean to minimize that. You yielded your opinions here and I know that wasn't easy. But whose opinions did you yield to, after all? Richard's and Wendy's?

KEITH: Whose else?

NARRATOR: I don't know. Mr. Nelson's, maybe. Mrs. Norris. All the boys who have free access to the family car. All the girls you approve of who keep late hours. The crowd.

EDNA: Oh, I see what you're driving at. Well, let me tell you, the first thing you'll learn as a parent is that your child has to live with his contemporaries.

KEITH: And you can't buck that.

NARRATOR: There's a lot of pressure, eh?

EDNA: It's terrific.

NARRATOR: On Richard and Wendy.

KEITH: Any kid would rather die than be different. You're young enough to remember that.

NARRATOR: And that puts a lot of pressure on you.

KEITH: Sure.

NARRATOR: So what really happens is that you yield to the pressure they're getting, and you all topple like a row of dominoes—because you don't want to find yourself standing alone—and you call that giving your kids the freedom to find themselves. I wonder if that adds up?

KEITH: You mean you think we should have insisted on having our way?

NARRATOR: Oh, I don't know what you should have done, Keith. You're the father. I'm just trying to call the balls and strikes. But I think there's a time somewhere along the line where every man has to respect his son as a man and his daughter as a woman. He has to let them make their own choices even when he doesn't like it. Maybe you think if you let your kids do what their friends do, you've accomplished that. But what if they choose something you don't like, and their friends don't approve of either?

KEITH: I don't know.

EDNA: That hasn't happened yet.

NARRATOR: Let's try it. Let me call them back.

EDNA: No, wait—

KEITH: Why borrow trouble?

NARRATOR: What kind of man do you want your son to be, Keith?

KEITH: I don't have any pattern set up for him. I've always kind of hoped he'd want to be a lawyer. I only got a couple of years of college myself. But I think we can swing the whole thing all right for Richard . . .

EDNA: And Wendy, too. Though we might as well be frank about it. Marriage is the important thing for a girl.

NARRATOR: All right. It's night.

(Lights down. EDNA switches on the lamp, and the NARRATOR moves to a watching position. In these playback scenes the characters lose all awareness of the NARRATOR who becomes merely an onlooker.)

NARRATOR: It's only a couple of weeks now before Richard leaves for college.

(KEITH stretches out on the sofa and falls asleep.)

NARRATOR: And Wendy is out—you know the boy, Edna. It's Fred.

(A frown gathers on EDNA's forehead, and she stands, as in front of a window looking out. She turns to her husband.)

EDNA: Keith. *(He doesn't stir)* Keith. For heaven's sake, Keith, why don't you get up and go to bed?

KEITH: *(Turning over)* All right.

EDNA: It's midnight, Keith.

KEITH: Oh. Do you want to go to bed then, dear?

EDNA: I'm waiting for Wendy.

KEITH: You can wait for her in bed.

EDNA: She's out with that boy, Fred.

KEITH: *(He sits up on the sofa and leans down to put on his shoes.)* I don't want Rich to work his first year in school.

EDNA: If he just made his own spending money—ten or fifteen dollars a week—it would help a lot.

KEITH: I think he's worried about college anyway. He's been looking worried about something. *(Starting out of the room.)* I don't want him to work for his first year— Good night.

EDNA: Keith . . . stay down here with me for a while, will you?
(He turns to look at her questioningly)
She's going steady with that boy.

KEITH: Who?

EDNA: Fred. She hasn't had a date with anyone else for almost a month.

KEITH: She's got a crush, eh?

EDNA: She's old enough to be thinking about marriage, you know.

KEITH: Oh, Edna—

EDNA: She is not a little girl! Now you'd better start facing up to that.

KEITH: Well, I know that, darling, but she's not past puppy love yet—

EDNA: How do you know? We can keep calling it puppy love, and then one day when it's too late we'll find out it wasn't.

KEITH: I suppose that's bound to happen—someday.

EDNA: What if it happens now—with this boy? Keith, when a girl Wendy's age sees this much of a boy, anything can happen.

KEITH: Is there something wrong with this boy, Edna?

EDNA: He's not a boy. He's twenty-seven years old, and he's been married and divorced. Now that's a fine catch for Wendy, isn't it?
(Sound of slamming door)

KEITH: Is that Wendy?

EDNA: No, it's Richard. I want you to talk to her, Keith. Will you?

KEITH: Look, Edna, there hasn't been any talk about marriage, has there?

EDNA: Will you talk to her?

KEITH: I don't know—
(RICHARD enters from the kitchen)

RICHARD: Hi, what are you doing up?

KEITH: You're keeping kind of late hours, aren't you?

RICHARD: Been to the movies.

KEITH: Might as well enjoy yourself while you can. You're going to be up to your ears in books every night pretty soon.

RICHARD: *(Turning away evasively)* S'pose I will.

KEITH: Your mother and I have been talking, Rich, and we think we can manage to keep you in enough pocket money so you won't have to work.

RICHARD: I've always had a job of some kind in high school.

KEITH: Well, I don't want you to have to worry about anything but your schoolwork. Not the first year, anyway.

RICHARD: That's nice of you, Dad.

KEITH: What's the matter with you, Richard?

RICHARD: Nothing.

KEITH: We—, you act like there's something wrong.

RICHARD: Well, there isn't.

KEITH: I get the feeling you don't want to look me in the eyes.

RICHARD: Will you stop picking on me?

KEITH: Are you coming to bed, Mother?

EDNA: I'm going to wait up for Wendy.

KEITH: Good night.

RICHARD: Dad.

KEITH: What?

RICHARD: I don't want to go to college.

(KEITH *turns back into the room. He looks at* EDNA. *They look at Richard, who looks down and purses his lips.)*

KEITH: What do you mean you don't want to go to college?

RICHARD: Mean just what I said.

EDNA: Well, I don't understand—

KEITH: When did you decide this? How long have we been planning? And you're supposed to leave in two weeks.

EDNA: And now, all of a sudden, you don't want to go.

KEITH: What's the matter with you, Son?

RICHARD: Nothing's the matter with me. I just don't want to go.

KEITH: Why haven't I heard about this until now?

RICHARD: You've been so het-up about it, I didn't want to say **anything**. I never did want to go. I was going to anyway, because you want me to. But the closer it gets, the more I don't want to go.

KEITH: This is your future, you know, Rich, not mine.

RICHARD: That's the whole point.

EDNA: It isn't easy for us, Richard, to make it possible, you know.

KEITH: Every boy you run around with is going to be starting college this fall—

EDNA: And if you don't, believe me, you're going to regret it for the rest of your life.

KEITH: Give me one good reason, Rich, why you don't want to go.

RICHARD: I'm sick of school. I want to get a job. Bum around, maybe. Travel. I don't know. Anything but school.

KEITH: And where do you think that's going to get you?

RICHARD: Where's school going to get me?

EDNA: A degree.

KEITH: A decent job.

EDNA: And a better living.

RICHARD: I don't even know what I want to study.

KEITH: You're going to take a general course to begin with, and after a while you'll decide what you want.

EDNA: You won't have to settle on a major until your second year or so.

KEITH: Believe me, Rich, you'll be getting your nose to the old grindstone soon enough.

EDNA: Once you've started working, you'll always be working.

KEITH: Your mother and I know what we're talking about.

EDNA: These are going to be the best years of your life, Richard.

RICHARD: There's only one thing wrong with everything you say. I don't want to go, that's all. I'm not sure what I want to do.

KEITH: Well, you better want to go to school, Richard, because you're going to go.

RICHARD: Dad—

KEITH: If you think I'm going to let you toss away your future for a fast buck in a factory or something, you're wrong.

RICHARD: Look—

KEITH: I made up my mind before you were born that my son was going to be a college man, and that's you.

RICHARD: Mom—

EDNA: Don't appeal to me, Rich. I'm not going to help you.

KEITH: There's nothing more to talk about, Rich.

(A door slams. WENDY *enters.)*

WENDY: Well, what's the powwow?

RICHARD: Ask the boss. *(He runs offstage.)*

WENDY: What's the matter?

EDNA: Nothing.

WENDY: What'd he do?

KEITH: We'll talk about it in the morning, Wendy.

WENDY: Okay. I want to get to bed, anyway. We're driving out to the lake in the morning.

EDNA: Who are you going with?

WENDY: Fred. *(She starts off.)*

EDNA: Wendy.

WENDY: What?

EDNA: You're seeing a lot of that boy, aren't you?

WENDY: Seems like it.

EDNA: *(Lightly)* Is it serious?

WENDY: *(Embarrassed)* Oh, Mother. *(Shrugging)* I don't know. *(She starts off again.)*

EDNA: Wendy, we want to talk with you.

KEITH: Edna, I think we've had enough—

EDNA: Your father and I don't approve of this young man.

WENDY: What's wrong with him?

EDNA: I don't know that there's anything wrong with him. But we think you see him too much.

WENDY: Well, if I'm supposed to make sense out of that—

EDNA: Wendy, he's not a young man you'd want to get serious about, is he?

WENDY: I don't know. Why not?

EDNA: You've hardly seen anything of your friends since you've been going out with him. He's older than all of them. And he's not like them, is he?

WENDY: He's a very fine person.

EDNA: If you saw him just occasionally— Keith—

KEITH: Every third or fourth date, Wendy.

EDNA: Every couple of weeks.

WENDY: I like him better than that.

KEITH: If you'd go out with a lot of different boys, honey, you'd be able to tell better what you do like.

WENDY: But I know now.

EDNA: You're too young to get this thick with anyone.

WENDY: What do you mean "thick"?

EDNA: If you can't understand what we're saying—

WENDY: Every friend I've got goes steady—

EDNA: With boys in their own crowd.

KEITH: You'll have to trust our judgment.

WENDY: Are you telling me not to see him?

EDNA: You can see him once every couple of weeks. I think you better call off tomorrow.

WENDY: Mother—

EDNA: Let's not talk about it any more tonight.

WENDY: Daddy, please—

KEITH: Wendy, someday you'll understand. We're doing this for your good.

WENDY: I don't understand. And I won't understand. And I'm not going to stand for it, either. You're dictatorial!
(She runs off. EDNA and KEITH look at each other for a moment.)

EDNA: Do you feel like a tyrant?

KEITH: A little. Do you?

EDNA: We can't let them throw themselves away, Keith.

KEITH: Let's go to bed.
(EDNA snaps off the lamp. Darkness and then the lights come up with the characters in the same positions as before the playback.)

NARRATOR: It isn't always easy, then, to let them make their own choices.

KEITH: It isn't easy to dictate to them, either.

NARRATOR: I can see that. But just to clear up a point of a while ago, there is a leash, isn't there?

KEITH: There's a limit.

EDNA: What kind of parents would we be if we let them hurt themselves?

NARRATOR: That's what I wonder. What I wanted to know to begin with is how much freedom you really give your children to come into their own. You give them freedom to do what their contemporaries do, because you trust their good behavior.

But do you give them freedom of choice when what they want is what you consider unorthodox?

EDNA: Listen to me. I know. A girl can make a romantic mistake when she's young that she'll pay for through a lifetime.

KEITH: And a boy can throw away his best opportunities because he doesn't know what he's doing.

EDNA: I didn't bear my children to be unhappy.

NARRATOR: There must come a time when their happiness isn't in your hands any more.

KEITH: Not yet.

NARRATOR: When does the time come, then, to let go and say their destiny is in God's hands and not yours?

KEITH: When they're wise enough to make the right choices.

NARRATOR: Then somewhere they have to learn to make significant choices for themselves and bear the responsibility for them.

EDNA: Even if they're wrong?

NARRATOR: We all have our right to failure. When does the time come when your concern is excessive, and your protection is overprotective? When do your children have to learn to flex the muscles of their own judgment, even if they take the wrong course and it breaks your heart? The time must come because if they can't stand against you and against the crowd on positions they take for themselves, then how do they become men and women? How do they become anything more than well-behaved children?

KEITH: Then what are parents for?

NARRATOR: To guide, to teach—remembering always that your children's destiny is not at any point in your hands, but in the hands of God. If you have realized this, then it seems to me you'll never have to face the question of when to let go. The hardest part of being a parent must be the initial decision— what it takes is faith. But if you don't want stunted children —try it—play the scene again. It's night. *(The lights go down.* EDNA *switches on the lamp.)* Wendy has her date with Fred tomorrow. Richard has told you his decision about school. They're upstairs now—

(EDNA *and* KEITH *stand for a moment, as if uncertain of what to do or unwilling to begin.)*

KEITH: I'll call him down.

EDNA: No. Wait a minute, Keith.

(She stands tense a moment, trying to brace herself, and then turns to speak off the set in the direction of the NARRATOR.)

EDNA: I can't do it!

KEITH: Edna—

EDNA: They don't know what they're doing. They're only kids. I can't just stand by—I can't let them, Keith. I can't.

KEITH: We'll try to reason with them—

EDNA: We have tried.

KEITH: Life isn't over, Edna. Maybe, somehow, they know better than we do—

EDNA: That isn't so. You know that isn't so. You go. You talk with them. I can't. *(She takes a seat on the sofa and* KEITH *sits beside her.)* So foolish. So headstrong.

KEITH: Maybe Richard needs a while to find his direction. He can start to school next year. Or the year after that, even.

EDNA: And it's just as possible that he'll never get there.

KEITH: And we can still influence Wendy. She isn't married yet.

EDNA: Not yet. Oh, Keith—to just sit on the sidelines and watch them make such mistakes. They're still my little children. I don't want to let them go, Keith—not yet—not yet —not yet—

(EDNA *cries, quietly.* KEITH *comforts her.)*

(The NARRATOR *addresses the audience)*

NARRATOR: Sometime it has to be said, "This child is an individual soul, the co-equal of mine." Sometime it has to happen. A child struggles for his independence and his maturity, and his right to make even wrong choices. Ultimately he must put his faith and trust, not in his parents, but in God. And for a parent this may be very hard and very painful. But to protect his child too long—that must be to stand between the child and God. For even as the parent bears alone the responsibility for his life and his choices before God, so is the child born with that privilege and that burden.

Curtain

PRODUCTION NOTES

The Set The set is somewhat more conventional and complete than the sets used in the other plays of "The Seeking Years" series. It consists of two areas: living room and kitchen, placed side by side and separated by a doorframe. The kitchen contains a small table and two chairs, one up center, the other stage left, and a counter or work area. In the TV production this last consisted of a set piece containing a sink and kitchen counter. A long table could be substituted, provided it gives the flavor of a kitchen. The living room contains a sofa (large enough for the father to lie down upon), placed down center and raked upstage, a telephone table upstage above this, and to the left a stair unit of at least three steps. In addition there should be an easy chair and lamp downstage left.

Exits Two exits are essential. One is the doorframe between the kitchen and living room, placed to the right, two or three feet from the telephone stand. This area should not be cramped. The other exit is a doorframe left of the step unit. This is a door to the outside. There can be a third exit, if desired, from the wings at stage left.

Props Four long leather straps, a newspaper, and string beans or similar vegetables.

Costumes For WENDY, casual clothes, with a change to party dress.

For RICHARD, sport clothes, with a change to a suit.

For EDNA, a house dress, with a change, if desired, to a bathrobe.

For KEITH, a suit.

Sound Effect An offstage door close.

THE PUZZLE

By Clair Roskam

originally broadcast
June 16, 1957

The cast:

JACK_____Richard Bright

KEN_____Thomas Walsh

FRANCES_____Sally Singer

MR. TURRELL_____Howard Wierum

NARRATOR_____Donald Symington

DIRECTED BY _____James MacAllen

SCENE

As the curtain rises, a man, the NARRATOR, *speaks directly to the audience:*

NARRATOR: Here is a puzzle. I give you a boy—he can be anywhere from fourteen to twenty years of age. Let's say he's eighteen and call him Jack, for convenience. You'll know him by his clothes—
> (*The lights come up on* JACK. *He is sitting very still astraddle a chair, his arms encircling its back and his head bowed. He is in profile to the audience, and is in shadow.*)

Switchblade knife and motorcycle are optional and not shown here. And as you may have guessed, he's in trouble.
> (MR. TURRELL *enters a distance behind* JACK *and the* NARRATOR. *He is a man in his fifties.*)

MR. TURRELL: And he always will be.

NARRATOR: Mr. Turrell. A druggist who employs Jack part time.

MR. TURRELL: He's antisocial. And incurable.
> (KEN *enters. He is a young man in his middle twenties. He stands near* MR. TURRELL.)

KEN: He's got to learn to use his head.

NARRATOR: Jack's brother, Ken.

KEN: He's smart enough not to get into jams like this.
> (FRANCES *enters. She is a girl* JACK's *age.*)

FRANCES: But I know why he does.

NARRATOR: Frances. Just a girl.

FRANCES: Because they provoke him to it.

NARRATOR: We all have our own ideas about a boy in a jam.
> (*Lights fade slowly on* MR. TURRELL, KEN, *and* FRANCES, *leaving only* JACK *and the* NARRATOR *lit.*)

NARRATOR: But as for Jack, he himself—and even to himself—is a puzzle. Jack isn't a real boy. I imagined him one day as I was thinking about a saying of the ancient philosophers. The saying is something to the effect that young men would rather do a thing because it is honorable than because it is useful. And I wondered how that could apply to a young man whose actions are generally thought to be dishonorable. A young man like Jack—a young man in trouble. How does he deal with it—most of all how does he deal with his sins and limitations and his sense of honor?

(JACK *raises his head and speaks.*)

JACK: I don't know what you're talking about.

NARRATOR: I'm wondering what you're thinking about.

JACK: I'm not thinking. I'm waiting.

NARRATOR: For what?

JACK: For someone to lower the boom.

NARRATOR: Well, relax, Jack. It won't happen for a while, anyway. You still have time to think.

JACK: I don't need time to think yet. When I see what's going to happen, then I got to think.

NARRATOR: Think about what has happened then.

JACK: I did that.

NARRATOR: What did you think?

(JACK *studies him for a moment and then rises suddenly from his chair, deciding to talk.*)

JACK: First thing I thought was, keep your mouth shut. Play it cool 'til you can talk with Ken—that's my brother. But old man Turrell was blowing his stack—Turrell's who I work for. At the drugstore. I don't know if you got the story.

NARRATOR: Tell it.

JACK: I work the fountain every afternoon after school and watch the store if he's in the back or out somewhere for a while. I been there for six months now. So this one day the fountain was real busy, see? I was flying around to keep up, and Turrell was s'posed to be next door or down the street or someplace. He went out the front door, see? Then all of a sudden the store gets quiet, and I'm taking a break when up he comes from the back of the store, sneakin' on his toes like a cat—

(*Lights go up on* MR. TURRELL, *standing behind them.*)

MR. TURRELL: Now, wait a minute—

NARRATOR: Go on.

JACK: And he scares me, see?

MR. TURRELL: You had good reason to be scared.

JACK: Who wouldn't be scared?

MR. TURRELL: That's the excuse he's hanging on to. He's supposed to have been too scared to give a straight answer—

(*Lights go up on* KEN *standing near* MR. TURRELL.)

KEN: Well, it makes sense to me.

MR. TURRELL: I come in and ask a simple question—

KEN: Simple question like, "How much are you stealing?" Right
out of the blue. That'd shake anybody, wouldn't it?

MR. TURRELL: Look, I gave that boy a lot of rope—

(*Lights up on* FRANCES, *standing on the other side of* MR.
TURRELL.)

FRANCES: To hang him.

KEN: Let's try to be reasonable for a minute.

MR. TURRELL: I've been more than that. I've been generous.

FRANCES: It isn't very generous to sneak around spying on
someone.

TURRELL: Am I supposed to hang a bell on my neck to walk
around my own store? I've got my interest to protect.

KEN: We can clear this up quietly, you know.

(*The following speeches of* TURRELL, KEN *and* FRANCES
are all spoken simultaneously down to the NARRATOR'S
interruption.)

TURRELL: That boy's a delinquent. You let him out of this and
you're going to have a convict on your hands—a menace! The
time to straighten him out is now. They've got a correction
school for kids like that—

KEN: It's not going to do you or anybody else any good to make
a racket over this. You can do the kid a lot of harm. Now,
come on, Turrell, let's face it—if you turn him over to the
cops, what have you got? Co-operate a little and we'll make
it up to you—

FRANCES: You want to know my opinion? I'll tell you. You brought this on yourself. Go around suspecting someone all the time and you get what you're looking for. If you ever thought to really trust Jack, he wouldn't let you down—

NARRATOR: Hold it. Hold it a minute.

(*They quiet suddenly.*)

Everybody's going to get a chance. But Jack is the issue here. Leave it to him.

(*The lights begin to fade on the trio.*)

Leave it to Jack for a while.

(*The lights go out on the trio. The* NARRATOR *turns to* JACK.)

JACK: So he comes in and he says he's been watching from the back and he sees I haven't been ringing up the sodas. I've been slipping the cash in my jeans. All right. I been too busy, see? The place was a riot. And then I forgot. But he jumps on me like that. "Where's the money?" he says, and right away I get scared and I don't know what he's talking about. So I stumble around and that makes me look guilty, see? And all the time I keep thinking I got to see Ken. I got to get to Ken. And Mr. Turrell keeps raving at me 'til I can't take it any more, so I tear out of the place.

NARRATOR: To see your brother?

JACK: That's right.

NARRATOR: Show me how that went.

JACK: I can tell you.

NARRATOR: I'd rather you played it out.

JACK: Ken's got a piece of a garage just a few blocks away. And I run right down there to see him. (JACK *moves as he talks, to a fragmentary setting of a garage office.* KEN, *when we next see him, is dressed in grease-stained white coveralls and a cap. He is on the telephone.*) Mr. Turrell called by the time I got there. If anything comes up, you see, people got a habit—well, my folks don't take so much interest, I guess—they got a habit of calling Ken about anything that has to do with me.

KEN: (*Into the phone.*) Okay—okay—yes, Mr. Turrell . . . (ad lib.)

(*He sets down the phone and turns to his brother in the doorway.*)

Well? Is it true or isn't it?

JACK: What do you think?

KEN: I don't know.

JACK: You going to help me or aren't you?

KEN: Sure, I'm going to help you.

JACK: What are you going to do?

KEN: I'm going to tell you something first, Kid. You can pile up so much trouble, you know, and pretty soon it gets too thick to get out from under.

JACK: Okay.

KEN: You're going to get a reputation for yourself. In fact, you've got one already.

JACK: Okay.

KEN: Going to get to a point where it doesn't matter whether you're right or you're wrong. If you're Jack Hesler, you're wrong, that's all.

JACK: All right!

KEN: Every time you get into a jam like this it gets tougher for me to get you out.

JACK: Look, are you going to help me or aren't you?

KEN: They've got a reform school in Baileyville, you know, and brother, you're skiddin' close—

JACK: (*Turning to leave.*) I'm not staying around for this—

KEN: Sit down!

JACK: (*Turning back, but not moving toward chair.*) If I want to listen to somebody blow, I could stay at the store—

KEN: It's about time you listened to something—

JACK: Well, I'm not going to do it—

KEN: Just shut up and sit down. (JACK *sits.*) You still got that money in your pocket? (JACK *nods.*) Let's see it.
　　(JACK *removes from his pocket a handful of change and a couple of bills which he lays on the desk.*)

KEN: Why don't you use your head?

JACK: What are you doing? Playing cops and robbers or something?

KEN: (*Counting the money.*) Almost four bucks. That's a big deal. If they send you to Baileyville you can brag how you got four bucks.

JACK: You ever figure there might be two sides to this story?

KEN: Turrell says he thought he saw you pull the same thing yesterday—

JACK: Let him prove it.

KEN: So he hung around today to make sure.

JACK: You know what he hangs around for? So if he sees me making myself a soda he can dock me. So if I drink a coke or something he can dock me.

KEN: Okay.

JACK: You know what I get for nothing down there? All the water I want.

KEN: Okay.

JACK: But I got to be careful with the ice.

KEN: He didn't catch you drinking a soda.

JACK: Yeah, he did. He forgot about it, that's all. He'll remember, don't worry. It'll come up. Just wait. "That kid was sneaking himself a soda!"

KEN: Okay, let's stick to the point.

JACK: That is the point, right there. You know what I make down there? A little more than half what the last guy got. 'Cause he's got me over a barrel. I had a hard time getting a job after that Stellmacher scrape, and he knew he could get me cheap. That's the point.

KEN: The point is he caught you taking four bucks.

JACK: The point is he's a thievin', tight-fisted old phoney, and he's got a guilty conscience. That's the point.

KEN: He caught you red-handed, Jack.

JACK: I explained it. Have you got any interest in my side of the story? Do you want to hear what I've got to say?

KEN: I already heard it. He told me. And I don't buy it. Now let's talk, shall we? You're in a jam and I'm trying to help. If this gets to the cops, it's going to be rough. You can pull this kind of dumb trick once too often, you know. What are you trying to do? Mess yourself up?

JACK: What are you trying to do? Get something off your chest ravin' at me?

KEN: You got a history of this stuff, you know.

JACK: What about you? Snow white, eh? Brother! Anybody ever got the tip on how you juggle your taxes, or how you chiseled yourself a piece of this dump—

KEN: You better pipe down—

JACK: Sure. You and Turrell, you ought to be partners. You want to raise Cain with me 'cause you find four bucks in my pockets—the poor saps that bring their cars in here should get off that cheap.

KEN: Okay, Jack. Point out the time I got in a jam. Point it out. Go ahead.

JACK: So you never got in a jam, so what? You're not lily white either. And if I got to hear any more Sunday school lessons from you or Turrell, I'm going to gag. You want to help me out now, or you want to yak for a while? (*He turns suddenly out of the scene to the* NARRATOR.) You want to know what I was thinking, Mister?

NARRATOR: I'd like to know what you were thinking, Jack.

JACK: I'll tell you what I was thinking—

KEN: Hey, wait a minute. We're going to play this out.

JACK: What for? He wants to know what I was thinking. He doesn't want to hear any more sermons from you.

KEN: He's riled up again, that's all. Let's play it out. He calms down in a minute.

JACK: Yeah, I calm down.

KEN: He apologizes to me, see? All that stuff about chiseling the customers and cheating on taxes—come on, play it out, Jack.

JACK: I don't want to play it out. Look, Mister, do I have to play it out?

NARRATOR: Just tell me what you were thinking.

KEN: He takes all that stuff back, see, 'cause it doesn't wash anyway—

JACK: I decide to play it smart and shut up, 'fore he gets mad and won't help me out with Turrell. I just sit still and listen while he preaches. I play it cool. "Yeah, Ken." "No, Ken." "Sure, Ken." Whatever he wants, see? But that's not what I was thinking. I was thinking, "Why, you crumb. If I took four bucks—if I *did* take four lousy bucks—that's nothing, *nothing* to what you cop every day. You and Turrell, both of you. Except you're smart and you keep clean and no one can prove anything."

NARRATOR: And how does that make you feel, Jack? Better?

JACK: No. It makes me feel stupid. All the scrapes I've been in. And what'd I ever get? Booted around and yelled at, that's all. Look at those guys. They're fat. There's the moral of it, I say to myself.

NARRATOR: What's the moral?

JACK: Keep clean and look for the angles and get rich. And don't let yourself be fall guy for every crook that wants to kick someone around 'cause he feels like a louse, 'cause he is a louse. That's the moral of it.

NARRATOR: In other words, be careful.

JACK: That's right.

NARRATOR: Is that the way you feel about it now?

JACK: I don't know.

KEN: Look, can I get a word in here?

NARRATOR: Sure, go ahead, Ken.

KEN: This kid has been in a lot of scrapes the last few years. I don't know what's the matter with him. When he was thirteen years old, he's with a gang that breaks into a grocery store. Yeah. Thirteen. Then there's speeding on that motorcycle of his, drinking, cheating at school, and a couple of years ago housebreaking—that's the Stellmacher thing he mentioned. Just out of one mess and into another. I lose my patience. You can understand that, can't you?

NARRATOR: I think I can.

KEN: Maybe I'm a little rough on him. But I always get him out, anyway. I don't know if he took that four bucks or not. He's been with Turrell for six months. Maybe he took four hundred by now. The main thing is, when you've got a record behind you like Jack, work it out and keep it quiet. I try to reason with him a little, that's all. There's no advantage in letting anyone know if there's some way around it. And I know the way.

NARRATOR: What's the way?

KEN: Admit he took the four bucks—

JACK: I'm not admitting anything.

KEN: Or twenty, or fifty, even. I offer to pay it back, plus, if Turrell's willing to forget it. The main thing is to keep it quiet. Look, we all make mistakes. We all cut a corner somewhere.

NARRATOR: That's the way you were thinking a minute ago, wasn't it, Jack? Assume everyone is doing more or less the same, so the wise thing is to wiggle out the best you can and be more careful in the future.

JACK: I *was* thinking that.

(*The lights suddenly go up on* TURRELL.)

TURRELL: And that's *my* point. Am I allowed to say something now? I've been standing here listening to a lot of ugly remarks—

NARRATOR: Yes, Mr. Turrell. Please.

TURRELL: There are two things in particular I want to point out here, young man. In the first place, I want to call attention to the attitude these boys have got. There's only one word for it—cynical. Not one hour after Jack runs out of the store he comes back with his brother, Kenneth. Now they try to tell me that the whole thing's a mistake. I scared him, you see—that's how they tell it—when I came in from the back. Now in the confusion and all, he's supposed to have got so mixed up that he tells me he hasn't got any money in his pocket, when I know he has and he knows he has, too.

KEN (*To the* NARRATOR): That's not hard to understand, is it?

TURRELL: Just wait a minute. This young man's been kind enough to give me some time, and I'm going to take it. Now, personally, I find that story pretty hard to swallow. But I'm willing to listen, until the next thing he tells me—Kenneth, here, the older boy—is that he's willing to pay back the money. Up to *fifty* dollars! Now you get that, don't you? He's going to pay back money that he swears the boy never took in the first place. What'd you make of that?

KEN: All I want is to keep the kid's record clean.

TURRELL: Makes me think, if he's willing to shell out fifty like that, maybe fifty's only a drop in the bucket. How am I supposed to know?

KEN: How does anybody know? As far as I know he never took a dime off you, and never meant to, either. If he was a kid that never had any trouble, you'd take his word and forget it. But as it is, if you turn him over to Kibbee—

TURRELL: Tom Kibbee, that's our chief of police here.

KEN: You're going to get him in a real mess he may never get out of. And what's that going to get you? I'm offering you fifty you never lost anyway, the kid gets off and you show a profit. What's wrong with that?

TURRELL: Well, I'll tell you. That just happens to bring up my second point here. Just about six months ago you came into the store looking for a job. You remember that day, Jack?

JACK: Sure.

TURRELL: Well, there was nothing in my window and nothing in the paper, either, about my needing help. I wasn't looking for help the day you came in. (*To the* NARRATOR) That's pretty important, here. And I'd just like it if you'd ask him if he's got any recollection at all of what was said between him and me that afternoon.

NARRATOR: I'd like you both to play it out.

(*The lights follow* TURRELL *as he moves to a fragmentary setting of a drugstore.*)

TURRELL: Well, it was on a Monday, if I recollect right. I remember there wasn't any business to speak of, and I was cleaning up the fountain myself. I said to him right off, "What makes you think I'm looking for help?"

JACK (*Who has joined him in the setting*): You haven't got anybody, have you?

TURRELL: Nope. Not now I haven't. I couldn't find anybody that worked out very well after the last fellow left, and I've been finding out I can take care of it pretty well by myself.

JACK: Be nice to have somebody you could depend on though. Look after the place if you want to go out. Sweep up the floor, and all that.

TURRELL: You ever worked a fountain?

JACK: No.

TURRELL: Well, there you see. I'd have to teach you everything and by the time you got it down pat, you'd be itching to do something else. I know you kids.

JACK: I'll stick 'til school's out anyway, I promise you that.

TURRELL: There's a lot of jobs around, you know.

JACK: I haven't found anything.

TURRELL: How hard you looked?

JACK: Pretty hard. I can't find anything to suit me.

TURRELL: Well, I'm sorry, my boy. The business I've been having doesn't justify it right now. Maybe come summer—

JACK: If you get a kid in here working the fountain, that brings a lot of kids in, you know, Mr. Turrell. I got friends that hang out at Guddat's now, for example, that more'n likely would start bringing their business in here.

TURRELL: Well, I'll tell you——what's your name, Son?

JACK: Jack.

TURRELL: Jack what?

JACK: Jack Hesler.

TURRELL: Well, I'll tell you, Jack—Hesler?

JACK: That's right.

TURRELL: Oh.

JACK: What'd you mean "Oh"?

TURRELL: Jack Hesler, eh? That's the same Hesler that paid a visit to the Stellmachers one night—

JACK (*Turning to leave*): Okay. Thanks anyway—

TURRELL: Well, wait a minute.

JACK: What'd you want?

TURRELL: What do *I* want? Did you come looking for a job or didn't you?

JACK: We've been through that.

TURRELL: Well, come on back here now and let's talk about it. (JACK *moves back.*) Might as well talk about it over a soda. What do you like? Chocolate or strawberry?

JACK: Okay.

TURRELL: Which?

JACK: Chocolate's okay.

TURRELL (*Making the soda*): I take it you've been having a hard time finding anybody that wants to take you on, eh? Eh? Well, come on. If we're going to do business we might as well talk about the facts.

JACK: Yeah. That's right. I've been having a hard time.

TURRELL: I can imagine. That was quite a thing breaking into those people's house. How you missed taking a trip to Baileyville's what mystifies me. How'd you get out of that anyway?

JACK: Are we going to talk about a job, or you just want to chat for a while?

TURRELL: Now take it easy, my boy. If a man's taking someone into his store, he wants to know what he's getting.

JACK: Okay, Okay. I been getting this line for so long—look, give it to me straight. Are you really thinking about giving me some work or aren't you? I mean, no kidding.

TURRELL: I think it'd be fair to say I'm thinking about it.

JACK: Well, the Stellmachers didn't press any charges, see? My brother talked to 'em. But there was some—there was some damage, see? And I got to make it right—I got to make some money. I really need a job, Mr. Turrell.

TURRELL: Whatever made you do that, anyway?

JACK: I don't know. I must have been wild. I must have been out of my head. There was some drinking that night—if you don't mind, what I'm trying to do is forget about it, if anybody'd give me a chance.

TURRELL: You mean you've tamed down a little?

JACK: I tamed down considerable, Mr. Turrell. I can promise you that.

TURRELL: I don't know, my boy. Like I told you, I've been trying to get along here by myself and save the money. Business being how it is. But I can see the spot you're on, Son. Trying to clean up your reputation again. I'd like very much to give you a hand if I could—

(JACK *turns suddenly out of the scene to speak to the* NARRATOR.)

JACK (*Strongly*): Would you like to know what that line of baloney's building up to?

TURRELL: Am I going to get to finish here?

JACK: He's telling me how softhearted he is, see? Going to give me the big break—

TURRELL: He's cutting me off here 'fore I get to the very point I'm trying to make—

JACK: He's getting me cheap!

TURRELL: Now he's done it again, you see that? He breaks right in there before anybody else gets a chance to have their say—

JACK: They all get their say, don't they? They all got plenty to say.

NARRATOR: What about your say, Jack?

JACK: I ain't got nothing to say. (*He turns away.*)

TURRELL: The point I'm trying to make is, I gave that boy a chance. I couldn't afford anyone at all, but I gave that boy a chance.

NARRATOR: What about that, Jack?

TURRELL: If you can't trust him under conditions like that, when someone goes way out on a limb to help, then you can't ever trust him.

NARRATOR: I get your point, Mr. Turrell.

TURRELL: If I'm greedy for money enough to take advantage of a boy like that, then why don't I take the fifty dollars and forget it? That boy's a delinquent.

NARRATOR: Mr. Turrell—

TURRELL: They've got a correction school at Baileyville to take care of him—

(*The* NARRATOR *makes a slight gesture with his hand, whereupon the lights go out on* MR. TURRELL. *Then the* NARRATOR *turns to* JACK, *who leans on the drugstore fountain hiding his head.*)

NARRATOR: What are you thinking now, Jack?

(*As* JACK *answers, the lights go up on* FRANCES *seated in a lawn swing a distance behind him.*)

JACK: Thinking about a girl.

FRANCES: I'm thinking about you, too, Jack.

JACK: I'm tired of listening to all the gaff. Sometimes it's nice to have someone listen to me for a change.

NARRATOR: Does she listen?

JACK: Yeah.

NARRATOR: What do you talk about?

JACK: Me.

NARRATOR: I'd like to hear that. Let's try it. It's after you leave your brother and Mr. Turrell at the drugstore—everything is still up in the air. You walk home—but not straight home—you take a detour—

FRANCES: Are you going to come over, Jack? Or are you going to keep going in circles?

JACK (*Moving over to her*): I was just passing by.

FRANCES: Three times in the last half hour.

JACK: Must have been two other guys.

FRANCES: Make yourself comfortable.

JACK: No, I got to go.

FRANCES: Oh, sit down for a minute.

JACK: Your dad home?

FRANCES: No. (JACK *sits, relaxing, on the ground near her.*) What if he was?

JACK: Hmmmmmm? Nothing.

FRANCES: Well, what if he was? Why do you always want to know if my dad's home?

JACK: He doesn't like me hanging around, that's why.

FRANCES: Did he ever say anything?

JACK: He doesn't have to. He doesn't like it. Now don't give me a lot of bull. He doesn't like it, and I know it.

FRANCES: What's the matter with you?

JACK: There's nothing the matter with me. What'd you mean, what's the matter with me? There's nothing the matter with me. So drop it.

FRANCES: Wow!

JACK: Well, Judas Priest. Talk about picky. What's the matter with you? (*Pause.*) Got in a little fracas at the drugstore. (*Pause.*) You're looking at a man that's practically on his way to reform school.

FRANCES: What happened, Jack?

JACK: Ah, nothing. Turrell's got a bellyache, that's all. That guy—so help me—I was working the fountain after school, and for a half hour or so it was a madhouse, see? Who brought him all that business? Ask him that, will you? So I didn't get a chance to ring up the cash, and I stuffed it in my pocket and then I forgot it. Then Turrell comes in from the back, where he's been waiting and playing detective, and he starts screaming, "Thief, thief, thief!" Not so much mad, though— tickled—you know what I mean? He's crazy, that guy.

FRANCES: What's he going to do?

JACK: He's going to have me electrocuted, if he can do it. (*Pause.*) Might as well.

FRANCES: Oh, Jack—

JACK (*Rising*): I got to get home.

FRANCES: Don't you dare leave now.

JACK: I don't feel so very hot. I don't know what I'm doing here, anyway. I can't stay out of trouble, and that's all there is to it. I'm one of those guys.

FRANCES: You didn't intend to take the money.

JACK: Didn't I?

FRANCES: Did you?

JACK: I don't know. I been saying I didn't, and everybody else says I did. Take your pick. I don't even know myself any more. I can stand right here and tell you barefaced that I don't even know any more. It's like a thing I'd do, though, isn't it?

FRANCES: I don't blame you if you did. I don't. I'd do it myself out of spite.

JACK: What'd you mean?

FRANCES: They're always picking at you, aren't they? Mr. Turrell, your brother, at school, your folks, and the police even, everybody. Always looking at you with slit eyes to see what you're going to do next. Well, I wouldn't disappoint them.

JACK: I give 'em plenty of reason.

FRANCES: Well, why not? They love it, don't they? (*Crying.*) It's so darn unfair.

NARRATOR (*As he enters the set*): Frances—

FRANCES: He may be a puzzle to you, but he's not to me. If anybody ever thought of trusting him—really—if they ever expected something good out of him—

NARRATOR: We're trying to help him, now.

FRANCES: Do you want to know what the truth is? Everybody likes to have a bad boy around just to have someone to cluck at. I don't blame you, Jack. I don't blame you. I'd steal him blind!

(*She holds a rope of the swing with two hands and bows her head to them, crying, as the lights fade on the garden scene.* JACK *rises and crosses to his chair, sitting as before.*)

NARRATOR: How do you deal with your sins and limitations, Jack? What do you think?

JACK: I'm not thinking. I'm waiting.

NARRATOR: But whatever Turrell decides to do or not to do, what about you?

JACK: Whatever Turrell decides to do, that's everything. What'd you mean?

NARRATOR: You're not handing yourself over to him?

JACK: He's already got me.

NARRATOR: Not all of you. What about that sense of honor young men are supposed to feel so strongly?

JACK: Haven't got much of that left.

NARRATOR: I wonder.

JACK: You wonder? Do you know what you're talking about? Did you get the story or not? Honor? Judas! What's that?

NARRATOR: That's you, maybe. The best part of you.

JACK: Yeah, maybe. And maybe you're talking about two other guys. Look, Mister, I'm tired—

NARRATOR: What are you thinking?

JACK: What am I thinking! What am I thinking! Get off it, will you? I'm not thinking, I tell you.

NARRATOR: You've been thinking a lot.

JACK: And it did a lot of good, eh?

NARRATOR: Maybe you've been going in a circle.

JACK: Well, I'll tell you something. It feels like a circle—with a lid on. What'd you mean a circle?

NARRATOR: The first thing you think when you get into a jam is that everyone's out to get you—that everyone's cut from the same cloth, and your mistake was getting caught.

JACK: You got any argument with that?

NARRATOR: Not necessarily. Did you get any help from it? (JACK *doesn't answer.*) And the next thing you want to do is to forget everything that's happened. Blot it out. And start again.

JACK: Who's going to let you forget?

NARRATOR: Maybe that's the trouble with that. There'll always be someone who likes to remind you.

JACK: I can name about fifty people without even thinking.

NARRATOR: And finally you get to feeling sorry for yourself. Feeling put upon and unworthy. Feeling like you're not as fit as good people. And all these things you feel and think are like moving in a circle, aren't they, Jack?

JACK: Why?

NARRATOR: Because you keep looking to other people to justify yourself, or to forgive you for the past, or to compare yourself with. And they seem to let you down, these other people. Why do you need to rely on anyone else?

JACK: What have I got to rely on?

NARRATOR: Maybe if you trusted all your shame and failure to God, maybe if you looked inside yourself and found what God gave you and loves there, maybe you'd forgive yourself, as he does, and find yourself. Maybe once you do that—your human relationships would change too. Maybe then you could look at other people as equals—as friends. But it's up to you to start the ball rolling. Because if you have to rely on others to forgive you and find you worthy, you may have a long wait before the saint comes along who's up to that.

JACK: It's pretty late in the day already, isn't it? They got me trapped.

NARRATOR: Do you think so? I wonder if we're ever really trapped? I wonder if we can't always break out of the circle. Who is it up to? (*The lights go up on* KEN, TURRELL *and* FRANCES, *standing behind them.*) Them? Which one, Jack? Now that you're in trouble. Is it your brother you want to pull you out? Will that help you find yourself and your worth? Or would you rather throw yourself on Mr. Turrell's mercy? And if he forgives you, will that take the load off your back? Or is it Frances you want to justify you and give you pity? Where does a young man find himself and his honor? Perhaps it's a matter only between him and God! It's up to you to decide, of course. I was only wondering.

(*The lights fade out.*)

Curtain

PRODUCTION NOTES

The Set There are five playing areas in this script, two of them
limbo areas, the others representing a garage office, a drugstore
soda fountain, and a backyard swing. These last three can be
as simply or as fully dressed as facilities allow. The chair
area, in which the play opens, is down center, lighted by a
single spot. Directly upstage is another limbo area, lighted
more broadly, for the other three actors. Down right is the
garage area, containing at least a desk and two chairs. (A
display of cans of oil, tires, or similar garage merchandise will
help to set this.) Down left raked is the drugstore soda fountain, which can be as simple as a counter and three stools, or
as elaborate as the real thing. Upstage and left of center is
the backyard swing; it should be placed so that the lights
from the upstage limbo area will not spill into it.

Costumes For JACK: jeans or black denim trousers, T-shirt or
sweat shirt, black leather jacket.

For MR. TURRELL: an ordinary business suit, or a white coat.

For KEN: a business suit, and a change to work clothes, or as
in the script.

For FRANCES: a dress, or skirt and sweater.

Props A phone, three dollar bills and change, a cleaning cloth,
a chocolate soda.

A THING OF BEAUTY

By Howard Rodman

originally broadcast
July 7, 1957

The cast:

BEATRICE_____.Diana Van Der Vlis

ALICE_____.Sarah Marshall

DOLORES_____Bryarly Lee

BAILEY_____.Pat Welch

ALEX_____George Grizzard

GREY_____Stephen Joyce

NARRATOR_____Donald Symington

DIRECTED BY _____James MacAllen

SCENE

A larger-than-life-sized poster, standing in limbo. The poster is of the type often used to promote motion pictures. It has one main feature: an idealized representation of a beautiful girl. BAILEY is painting. ALEX and GREY watch. The NARRATOR crosses onto the stage, and addresses the audience.

NARRATOR: This is the story of a search made on a college campus: a search for beauty. And since, as the poets say, "Beauty is truth, truth beauty; that's all ye know on earth, and all ye need to know"—this is also the story of a search for truth. *(He turns to the students.)* Gentlemen, who is this girl?

ALEX: This is the girl of our dreams.

GREY: This is the girl we're looking for.

NARRATOR: Where does she come from?

BAILEY: Alex told you: she's the girl of our dreams. They told me to make a picture of the most beautiful girl in the world. They described her to me in detail: thirty-seven, twenty-four, thirty-six—chest, waist, and hips in that order. Make this picture, they said to me, and we'll find a real girl to fit it. And that's what I did.

ALEX: We told Bailey the color of her eyes, the shape of her lips, the color and texture of her hair. We described the symmetry of her teeth, and the proportions of her legs with respect to thickness of calves and ankles.

GREY: We told Bailey of the gentle rosy tints of her skin and of her tapering fingers.

BAILEY: And I made it the way they said.

NARRATOR: And now you're going to find a girl to fit those specifications?

ALL: Exactly.

NARRATOR: And when you find her, what do you do then?

75

BAILEY: Why, we'll have the most beautiful girl in the world, and we'll all fall in love with her.

ALEX: She'll probably get a movie contract. We're giving this a lot of publicity.

GREY: Look!

> (GREY *unfurls a sheet of paper he carries rolled in his hand. He smooths it out onto one side of the poster and it sticks there. It reads):*

Are you as beautiful as she? Do you dare admit it? Call Crestville 1-1111.

ALEX: You see? It's a contest!

BAILEY: We rented a special phone for the occasion. Everything is going to be very businesslike.

GREY: The contest is open to every girl on the campus. Absolutely fair.

> (*The three male students stare at their masterpiece a moment longer, then as the bell rings to signal beginning of classes, they shake hands and dash off. The* NARRATOR *faces the audience again.)*

NARRATOR: And so, now that we understand the contest, we can proceed with our story.

> (*Three female students come by, each dressed identically in a typical college girl's costume. They stop and look at the poster. Although the three girls are dressed identically, each is different:* BEATRICE *is a raving beauty.* ALICE *is attractive, no more.* DOLORES *is plain. They gaze at the poster, each reacting in her own way.)*

NARRATOR: A million cars may be made out of a single mold, each one identical with the other. A million homes may be built on a single plan, each shaped identically with the others. A frying pan and a light bulb may be duplicated in an infinite series. But human beings present a problem in this area—for each one is different in shape, manner, mind, and spirit. And yet, it almost seems as if we are ashamed of this, for our young people, particularly, take great pains to seem as like each other as they can.

> (*The three girls never take their eyes off the poster as they talk.)*

DOLORES: She's very beautiful.

ALICE: A little artificial. Don't you think?

DOLORES: Just very beautiful.

(BEATRICE *takes a pad and pencil from her purse and notes the telephone number. Noting this,* ALICE *copies the phone number for herself. And* DOLORES, *not wishing to be left out, finally makes a note of it on the inside cover of a textbook. Then, without another word of discussion, the three girls leave.*)

NARRATOR: And so (*indicating the poster*), we have the ideal. And now we must examine the reality. For this we need a mirror. (*Talks as he crosses away from the poster, through limbo, to the mirror.*) For we need to know how each sees herself.

(*The mirror is simply a frame, and each girl stands behind it, as we observe as if we were the girl and the girl within the frame is merely a reflection.* BEATRICE *crosses behind the mirror.*)

NARRATOR (*To* BEATRICE): Good morning.

BEATRICE: Good morning.

NARRATOR: You're going to enter the contest, aren't you?

BEATRICE: Yes. I'm going to win it.

NARRATOR: Why are you so sure?

BEATRICE: Look at me. Can't you see how beautiful I am?

NARRATOR: Isn't there anyone who's more beautiful than you are?

BEATRICE: There can't be!

NARRATOR: Why not?

BEATRICE: Because that's all I have!

(*She runs away. The frame is empty for a moment, then* ALICE *comes by, glances at it, is drawn back, looks at herself. She shakes her head, slightly.*)

NARRATOR: Good morning.

ALICE: Good morning.

NARRATOR: Are you going to enter the contest?

ALICE: Yes.

NARRATOR: Why? Do you think you'll win?

ALICE: No.

NARRATOR: Why are you going to enter, then?

ALICE: Did you ever take a chance on a raffle?

NARRATOR: Yes.

ALICE: Did you think you were going to win?

NARRATOR: Not particularly.

ALICE: Shall I judge myself in advance? Shall I say of myself
that I'm so unattractive that I have no chance to win? I will
not say that!

NARRATOR: But you've just said you don't think you'll win.

ALICE: Only to myself.

*(She departs abruptly. The frame is empty for a moment,
then* DOLORES *walks up to it out of the darkness.* DOLORES
*hangs her head and doesn't look into the mirror really.
Yet she stands before it.)*

NARRATOR: Good morning.

DOLORES: Good morning.

NARRATOR: Are you going to enter the contest, Dolores?

DOLORES: I have to.

NARRATOR: Do you think you'll win?

DOLORES *(Smiles wistfully):* How can you look at me and even
ask?

NARRATOR: Why are you going to enter, then?

DOLORES: Because a person has a right to think well of herself.
And it doesn't matter what anyone else thinks. A person has
a right to think of herself as beautiful, and wise, and witty
and desirable. And no one can take that away from you!

NARRATOR: Don't you like to look in the mirror?

DOLORES: Would you if you were me?

(DOLORES, never looking, walks away.)

ALEX *(offstage):* CR-1-1111 . . . All right, we'll send you an application form and you return it with a picture of yourself.
You're welcome.

*(The lights come up on the office area. There are a tele-
phone on a little table, two chairs and a card table.
BAILEY and GREY keep track of the calls. ALEX hangs up
and the phone rings again immediately.)*

ALEX: CR-1-1111. Yes, anyone can enter. Yes. Just send us a
picture of yourself along with the application. Who? . . .
Thank you.

(He hangs up and bursts into raucous laughter)

BAILEY: What's so funny?

ALEX: Dolores!

> (BAILEY *and* GREY *burst into laughter, whooping and slapping their thighs, at the image* ALEX *sums up with the face he makes when he mentions* DOLORES' *name.*)

NARRATOR: Good morning, gentlemen. Good morning, gentlemen. *(There is an irony in the accent he puts on the word "gentlemen" that sobers the three students up.)* How goes the contest?

ALEX: Perfect!

BAILEY: The most beautiful girls on campus!

ALEX: Some of them, anyway.

GREY: A hundred and two calls. We're a success.

ALEX: And more coming.

NARRATOR: Are you sure that the girl on the poster is beautiful?

ALL: Are you crazy!

BAILEY: Beautiful! She's out of this world!

GREY: Of course she's beautiful.

NARRATOR: In what sense?

ALEX: Look at her! Just look at her! In what sense do you mean "in what sense"?

NARRATOR: Is she kind? Is she good? Is she capable of giving love?

BAILEY: What are you talking about?

ALEX: That's just a picture!

NARRATOR: That's what I'm talking about. That's a picture; but what is it a picture of? Thirty-seven, twenty-four, thirty-six?

ALEX: He's out of his mind!

> *(The phone rings and* ALEX *answers.)*

ALEX *(Into phone):* CR-1-1111 . . . All right, we'll send you an application form. . . . Just fill it out and enclose a photograph of yourself.

> *(The conversation stops as the scene disappears and the* NARRATOR *crosses back to the poster. There is a small bench alongside and* BEATRICE *is sitting there.)*

NARRATOR: May I sit down?

(*He sits at a nod from* BEATRICE, *and stares at the poster.*)

BEATRICE: You're all alike.

NARRATOR: In what way?

BEATRICE: The way you look at girls. Hungry, and wanting what you see; and never caring what there is except what you see. I wish I'd been born ugly. Look at me. No, really look at me: not the color of my eyes or the shape of my nose or my lips—look at me! At *me!* I'm a girl and a person and I have a brain. Do you know that? Can you tell it by looking at me?

(DOLORES *begins to laugh offstage, and they turn their heads in her direction. She is standing just beside them and laughing.*)

BEATRICE: What are you laughing at?

DOLORES: Look at me. No, really look at me: not the color of my eyes or the shape of my nose or my lips—look at me! At *me!* I'm a girl and a person and I have a brain. Do you know that? Can you tell it by looking at me?

BEATRICE: Don't *you* make fun of *me!* Because when someone falls in love with you, it'll be for what you are and not what you look like!

DOLORES: Who? Who's going to look past what I look like? Men fall in love with beauty!

BEATRICE: No, they don't! They look at it and worship it and want it, but they never fall in love with it. They turn their backs on it in the end, because they don't trust it.

DOLORES: I'll trade places with you; here, now, tomorrow, next year. Trade places with me! Give me one day in my life to look like you!

BEATRICE: You don't know what you're saying. You don't know what agony it is to be like me!

DOLORES: Do you know what agony it is to be like me?

(DOLORES *turns away to hide her tears.* BEATRICE *turns away to hide her tears, and the lights go out on them leaving only the* NARRATOR *lit. He talks directly to the audience.*)

NARRATOR: And so it seems to go: another case of greener grass in the other fellow's yard, as the saying goes. And some questions must be asked here.

(GREY *enters the stage on a cross, but stops when the* NARRATOR *calls to him.*)

NARRATOR: Grey—

GREY: Yes?

NARRATOR: Grey, is Beatrice beautiful?

GREY: Yes.

NARRATOR: Is Dolores?

GREY: No.

NARRATOR: What does that mean?

GREY: It means that I would want a date with Beatrice, but I wouldn't want one with Dolores.

NARRATOR: Beatrice is beautiful and therefore you like her.

GREY: I don't like her at all. She's a snob for one thing, and she's not very bright for another thing.

NARRATOR: Why would you want to take her out, then?

GREY: Well, it's the thing to do. Everybody wants to go out with Bea; she's beautiful. It gives you a certain kind of distinction, you know.

NARRATOR: To go out with beautiful girls, you mean?

GREY: Yeah. It gives you prestige. Everybody says, "Hey, look who Grey's got for a date!"

NARRATOR: Do you like Dolores?

GREY: She's a nice kid.

NARRATOR: Do you ever go out with her?

GREY: I can't afford to. You know; you go out, everybody sees you; they say "Man, look at the beast Grey latched onto."

NARRATOR: Why do you date girls?

GREY: To have a good time.

NARRATOR: Can you have a good time with a girl you don't like?

GREY: You mean, like Bea? Well, it's a good time—in a way, I guess. It costs a lot of money. Believe me, that girl is used to having money spent on her. But once in a while, it's worth it.

NARRATOR: But do you have a good time?

GREY: Well, sure, it's all right. She's a good dancer; she's nice to look at; everybody sees you. Sure, it's a good time. Listen, I'll tell you the truth—there's half a dozen girls I'd rather go out with, but what's the percentage? If the girl's a little ugly, everybody thinks you haven't got what it takes.

NARRATOR: What does it take, Grey?

GREY: The best—nothing but the best!

NARRATOR: Are you the best, Grey?

GREY: Nobody asks that. They just ask if you go with the best. (*GREY exits. The* NARRATOR *gestures to the lighting man.*)

NARRATOR: Light up the picnic area, please.

(*The lights come up on a section of fence, beyond which is a small plot of grass.* ALICE *is sitting on the grass, a picnic lunch spread out before her on a tablecloth.* ALEX *is with her. The* NARRATOR *leans on the fence.*)

NARRATOR: There's a certain amount of pretense in everyone's life; pretense for the purpose of gaining social esteem. Men wear padded shoulders in their jackets to appear broader and stronger. Women's clothing is designed to pad the lines of the figure in one place, take it in in another. We pretend to have read books we haven't read. We like to think that we eat the socially esteemed foods: lobster thermidor sounds like a good dish to order when you're eating at a restaurant—it sounds impressive. And none of this, perhaps, is really bad. We don't really want a society in which somebody walks down Main Street in his underwear just to be different. Neither do we want a society where anyone will do anything just to be liked, just to be well regarded.

(*The* NARRATOR *exits and* ALICE *and* ALEX *begin their scene. They have apparently been having a spat, and for the moment they are not talking to each other.*)

ALICE (*Abruptly*): I'm not asking much.

ALEX: I can't do it, that's all!

ALICE: Yes, you can!

ALEX: Okay, I don't want to!

ALICE: That's more nearly true.

ALEX: What do you care who wins the crazy contest? Since when have you been nuts about being beautiful?

ALICE: I'm not asking to win. I'm just asking you to vote for me.

ALEX: Honey, you've got my vote all the time!

ALICE: I want it in public.

ALEX: Honey, there's three of us: there's me, there's Bailey, and there's Grey. What difference does it make if I vote for you? I'm just going to get outvoted. It's a beauty contest; it's all there; there's no opinion on the matter.

ALICE: I think there is an opinion. I want to know what you think of me.

ALEX: I'm nuts about you.

ALICE: And nuts about Beatrice, too?

ALEX: I don't know what gets into you girls. You're all the time burning about Beatrice! Who am I out here with? Beatrice or you? How much more answer do you want?

ALICE: I want a lot more answer than that.

ALEX: I can't vote for you. She's got the figure, she's got the face: everybody knows it. If I vote for you, I'll look like a fool. (ALICE *crosses away.*) Where are you going?

ALICE: I don't want you to look like a fool. And I don't want to look like a fool. I'm tired of getting dates after somebody calls Beatrice and finds out she's busy that night. I'm tired of answering the phone and hearing somebody say, "I know it's a little late in the day to ask what you're doing tonight, but what are you doing tonight?" I'm tired of being second best. I want to be me. I'll tell you what I want: I want somebody to look at me and think I'm the most beautiful girl who was ever born. Not beautiful compared to Beatrice, or Marilyn Monroe, but of myself beautiful. For what I am, and for what I have to give, and for what I mean to somebody.

ALEX: Listen—

ALICE: I don't want to listen—

(ALEX *is on his feet by now and is holding her.*)

ALEX: What's important about this whole thing? You put on twenty pounds or you take off twenty pounds and you look like a different girl! You dye your hair differently and you look like a different girl!

ALICE: It's important enough for you to run a contest about it!

ALEX Ah, come on, hon!

ALICE: Leave me alone!
(ALEX *tries to kiss her, but* ALICE *keeps turning her head away.*)

ALEX: Okay!

ALICE: Okay, what?

ALEX: Okay, you've got my vote.

ALICE: All right. But not for a kiss.

ALEX: No. Just because it means so much to you.
(*They look at each other for a moment and then* ALICE *kisses* ALEX, *and he kisses her hard in turn. The* NARRATOR *enters the picture. He gestures to the light man.*)

NARRATOR: Turn the lights out, please. The question still remains: why is winning this contest important? For Beatrice who knows she's beautiful without a contest—why? For Dolores, who knows she can't win—why? For Alice, who had to use coercion to get a vote—why? (*He calls*) Dolores?

DOLORES (*offstage*): Yes?

NARRATOR: Dolores, may I talk with you?
(*He crosses past the poster through darkness to another pool of light. There are a vanity and a mirror and a chair in front of it. There is a little stuffed toy on the vanity, and* DOLORES *is seated at the vanity. She has been experimenting with make-up, and has given herself exotic eyebrows and eye shadow, and picked her hair up, and is now working on her mouth.*)

DOLORES: (*With some sense of humor in what she is attempting*): It's a mess, isn't it?

NARRATOR: I like you better as yourself.

DOLORES (*Indicates the lipstick*): It's the latest shade. (*She sets the lipstick down.*) It really won't do the trick. I was talking to a boy today who's very good at photography. He says you can do almost anything with lights and shadows. I asked him if he'd take my picture and he said he'd be glad to. He said, with the right lighting, he could make me look like any movie star I want to pick out.

NARRATOR: Don't you have to be judged in person?

DOLORES: No, just the picture.

NARRATOR: But no matter what the picture looks like—let's say you won the contest—can you look like that picture day by day, by yourself?

DOLORES: They won't know. If everyone says my picture won the contest, then the next time people look at me, they won't dare say I look the way I do. They'll have to say how beautiful I am, because I won the contest.

NARRATOR: Your picture will have won.

DOLORES: My picture is me. Oh, don't torment me. I don't want to go through all this. I don't want to have to convince myself that I have a chance when I know I haven't got a chance. I don't have any choice, though, do I?

NARRATOR: Dolores, look at yourself. You're not ugly. Why do you keep saying you're ugly?

DOLORES: Don't you understand? I'm not in fashion any more. My type of girl went out in 1900. You have to have "chic." You have to have a certain air about you. Some have it and some don't. My hard luck—I was born fifty years too late. Do you know something strange? I would make a very good wife. And all the things that men want from a wife—I think I have all those things. But then they go look at the way a girl looks, you see. And that's the way they pick a wife. You see, if you have fingernails this long, then how can you wash dishes? Well, I suppose you can always get a dish-washer. But then if you happen to marry a man who can't afford to get you a dish-washer and you break your nails, he gets angry with you anyway.

NARRATOR (*Gently*): How do you know?

DOLORES: Because that's all they look at, the way you look. I told you ten times. You just don't believe me. That's all they look at. And if that's all they want and you break your fingernail, then they would have to be angry. I'm going to go down town and let this boy take a good photograph of me.
   (*She exits.*)

NARRATOR: (*He calls*): Beatrice?

BEATRICE: Come in. (*The lights come up.* BEATRICE *is seated in front of her vanity, her hands folded in her lap. She is wearing some kind of wrapper which conceals the fact that she is underdressed now in a bathing suit.*) Do you think I'm beautiful?

NARRATOR: Yes, I do.

BEATRICE: It's a lie.

NARRATOR: No, I'm telling the truth.

BEATRICE: Not what you think. What is. *(She hands him a snapshot which has been stuck into the frame which surrounds the mirror.)* Do you know who that is?

NARRATOR: Someone in your family?

BEATRICE: It's me: eight years ago. *(She takes the photo back and studies it.)* That's an ugly little girl, isn't it! I was born ugly. Oh, I knew it. Oh, I was made to feel it. Do you know what I did? When I finished high school, I went to a plastic surgeon. I had my nose made over, I had my jaw made over, I had my teeth capped. I dyed my hair. I dieted off thirty-seven pounds—thirty-seven pounds. Now look at me. I'm beautiful now, aren't I?

NARRATOR: You're very beautiful.

BEATRICE: I'm a fraud. I keep waiting for them to find out. I go out with a boy, and I keep looking in mirrors to see if anything has changed. Because it's not me: it's not me. But it doesn't matter. Nobody ever knows. Do you believe in God?

NARRATOR: Yes.

BEATRICE: Why did he make me so ugly? Why did he make me so ugly? Everything I do, all the hours I'm awake, all the hours when I should be sleeping, only one thing on my mind —to be beautiful. God did that to me.

NARRATOR: You did it to yourself, I think.

BEATRICE: God made me ugly!

NARRATOR: Were you ugly inside?

BEATRICE: Yes! Because I wanted to be loved and petted and spoiled like pretty little girls are. And even my mother and my father couldn't really look at me without wincing. Here! Look at it again! *(She thrusts the picture into his hands.)* I wanted to be a movie star. I would go to the movies and see the beautiful people on the screen. I would see the boys fix their eyes on a beautiful actress, yearning toward her, out of their seats toward the screen. Even the boys I went with sometimes. Even though it was dark and they couldn't see me. I read movie magazines, one after another. I read how stars aren't really born beautiful; their noses are fixed, and their hairlines are raised, their eyebrows are shaped. And I wanted to be like them. I wanted so to be like them. Beautiful.

NARRATOR: Do you know what beauty is?

BEATRICE: I'm beautiful. Look at me and you'll see. I get up at six in the morning and do exercise. I eat a lettuce leaf for lunch. I'm beautiful.

NARRATOR: Is that enough?

BEATRICE: No.

NARRATOR: Couldn't you have trusted God a little?

BEATRICE: No. He made me ugly.

NARRATOR: But he didn't make you beautiful, did he?

BEATRICE: No. I did that to myself.

(As the lights go out on BEATRICE, *a phone rings faintly in the distance. The lights go up on* ALICE *at one end of the phone: and on* ALEX, *on the other end of the phone.)*

ALEX: Hello.

ALICE: Alex—

ALEX: What's the matter?

ALICE: Nothing's the matter.

ALEX: You sound as if you were crying.

ALICE: Just a little. I feel so cheap. Alex, I don't want to be in that contest.

ALEX: I told you: I gave you my word. You've got my vote.

ALICE: Alex, do me a favor: tear that picture up, please! Please tear it up!

ALEX: Why?

ALICE: Do you love me?

ALEX: Yes, I love you.

ALICE: Then will you prove it? Will you tear that picture up?

ALEX: All right, if that's what you want.

ALICE: Thank you. I'll talk to you tomorrow. Good night.

(The lights go out on the two ends of the phone call. The light comes up on the NARRATOR.)

NARRATOR: It seems a kind of comedy, if there weren't so much hurt attached. That Beatrice, who is beautiful now, should forever have to prove she is not ugly. And that Dolores, who is not ugly, should forever have to prove her beauty. And that Grey should ask Beatrice out when he would prefer to be with Dolores, and that Dolores should never know. It seems a kind of comedy. And for what?

(BEATRICE *now enters the scene in a bathing suit, and wears a papier-mâché crown and a velvet mantle and carries a scepter.* DOLORES *comes behind and carries the train of the mantle, and* ALICE *watches. The three boys enter, too, as well as all the extras the budget will afford.* BEATRICE *stops and looks at the poster and then stands before it so that all can see how closely she resembles it.*)

BAILEY: We, the assembled, having duly examined and judged a lot of photos of a lot of girls, state to you, Beatrice Drake, that you most resemble the girl of our dreams, and we present you with this crown, and this scepter, and this mantle. And we present you with this document which says that you, Beatrice Drake, are a "thing of beauty"!

(All assembled cheer and applaud. BEATRICE *smiles. Then all motion stops, save for the* NARRATOR *and* BEATRICE.)

NARRATOR: Do you feel better about yourself now, Beatrice?

BEATRICE: I've won.

NARRATOR: Does that satisfy you?

BEATRICE: Dolores would like to be me, and Alice is envious.

NARRATOR: Does that make you content?

BEATRICE: He said, in front of everyone, that I'm a thing of beauty.

NARRATOR: And is that what you want?

BEATRICE: No. And if they knew, they would cry, wouldn't they? They would cry for me.

NARRATOR: Why would they cry, Beatrice?

BEATRICE: Can't you see? Don't you understand. A thing of beauty is still a thing, isn't it? I only want to be a woman.

(Then the movement on the part of the onlookers starts again. The NARRATOR *crosses away, the lights go out behind him, and the noise subsides, leaving him alone.)*

NARRATOR: This is a kind of game we play with each other. A rather cruel senseless kind of game in which false values are substituted for real. There are some who play another kind of game. They try to look beneath the deceptive exterior for the real person, to discover God's design and to encourage it into being. Either way, however, there is a warning and a promise we do well to remember: "Be careful what you set your heart upon, for it shall surely possess you."

Curtain

PRODUCTION NOTES

Mood The television production of this play made use of a limited amount of stylized movement, worked out by director John Desmond and actor-dancer Pat Welch, who played Bailey. In general, the stylization consisted of larger-than-life gestures for the boys (in the poster and office scenes) and dance movement for the girls (in the poster and mirror scenes). Beatrice's steps were rather broad and statuesque, Alice's were lyrical and more confined, Dolores' shy and diffident. Further, each girl had her own musical motif, echoing these same characteristics. The final parade and crowning of the winner was also performed with exaggerated movement, and played to a jazzy march.

The stylization was considered successful in the televised production; there seems to be no reason why a stage production should not use at least as much. The script runs a considerable gamut of mood, from high gaiety and excitement in the opening and office scenes, to considerable poignancy in the interviews with the girls and the telephone scene; stylization seemed to the producers to help in conveying the mood.

Sets The script calls for a minimum of five areas, which may be laid out as the director finds best. The following is a suggested pattern only:

1. At stage right an area with a bench, a fence, and a tree or other object against which the poster can be displayed. Here the poster, bench, and picnic scenes may be played.

2. Upstage from this a large, virtually life-sized cutout mirror frame in limbo.

3. Center stage, a large limbo area, for narrator, the telephone scene, and the final scene. About two feet down from this a baby spot, for the narrator's final scene with Beatrice and his closing.

4. Downstage left, a vanity with a cutout frame representing an oval mirror.

5. Upstage from this an office area with three chairs, a large desk, a typing table, and at least two phones on the set. Note that both the office set and the limbo, mirror, and vanity set may be removed after the scenes in which they are used.

NO MAN IS
AN ISLAND

*By James Benjamin
and Don Kellerman*

*based on an original story by
Helen Kroner*

*originally broadcast
July 21, 1957*

The cast:

GEORGE_____Bill Gunn

GEORGE'S GRANDFATHER____Frederick O'Neal

PAUL_____James Olson

PAUL'S FATHER_____Sheppard Strudwick

PHYLLIS_____Nancy Malone

COUNTERMAN_____Charles White

NARRATOR_____Donald Symington

DIRECTED BY_____James MacAllen

SCENE

The curtain opens on a dark stage with only the NARRATOR *spotlighted upstage. The light follows him as he moves downstage holding a small book. He closes it and speaks.*

NARRATOR: "No man is an island entire of itself; every man is a piece of the continent, a part of the main—any man's death diminishes me because I am involved in mankind and therefore never send to know for whom the bell tolls; it tolls for thee."

John Donne wrote those lines over 300 years ago and they ring just as true today as they did on the day he set them down. The question of man's relation to man is part of the infinitely greater question of man's relation to God. The "seeking years"—the growing years—are questioning years—and the questions that young men and women ask are a part of growing up.

We may not know the answers—but the questions must be faced. Today, as in John Donne's day, there are those who are islands unto themselves. Islands sometimes structured of ignorance—sometimes of fear of the unknown. Take this young man—

(The NARRATOR *snaps his fingers and a young man, with a puzzled expression on his face, appears in a pool of light, holding a letter.)* He should be happy. An old friend is coming to see him. A friend he made in the Army. It was a friendship based on proximity as much as anything else. But then most friendships are. And this one solidified on the basis of mutual interests—the law, music . . . and anxiety to get on with service-interrupted educations. *(Crosses to* PAUL*)* Have I been accurate? Is George your friend?

PAUL: He's one of the best friends I ever had. But his coming to this town, his going to school here . . . I hope it doesn't make a difference. Nothing like this has ever happened here.

NARRATOR: So we see it's the unknown that's bothering Paul. It's fear that begins digging gulfs—developing islands of separateness around each of the friends. *(Walking to area about to be lit.)* What is there about George's arrival that has shadowed his friend's brow? It's a simple thing *(snaps fingers— lighting another boy in a pool of light).* It's the color of his skin.

(The NARRATOR *walks between the two boys frozen in islandlike positions.)*

NARRATOR: Each of these young men has memories of the other, memories that go back to the time of their first meeting. Sift your memories, Paul—recall their first scene for us.

(The spot goes out on Paul.)

NARRATOR: . . . an Army barracks in an Army camp. And you, George. You're a soldier again . . .

(The lights go out on GEORGE *and the* NARRATOR *and almost immediately rise on a light fragmentary barracks set. Two cots facing each other. Two footlockers. A door from which* GEORGE *has stepped.* PAUL *sits on cot. Looks up.)*

GEORGE: Is this Dog Company—second platoon?

PAUL: Yeah. What can I do for you?

GEORGE: Oh, it's too late to do anything for me now. I'm supposed to bunk here. *(Moves in, laying gear on floor.)*

PAUL *(Half rising):* Here?

GEORGE: Yes, here. Why? Anything wrong?

PAUL: Oh, no. Nothing at all.

GEORGE: What kind of outfit is it?

PAUL: Just like any other. It has been.

GEORGE: What's the "Old Man" like?

PAUL: He's okay. Well—make yourself at home.

(He gets up—passes from set, leaving GEORGE *staring after him as the lights cross-fade from this set to an area just outside the "door" where the* NARRATOR *moves in to meet the exiting* PAUL.)*

NARRATOR: Was that the beginning of a friendship?

PAUL: That was the beginning of shame. You don't snub a man like that without feeling shame.

NARRATOR: You know that. You knew it then. What made you do it?

PAUL: There are some things you don't look at too closely. You can't because if you saw the things that moved you, sometimes you'd never look in the mirror again. I did it because I didn't know any better. I did it because the color of his skin jarred me—because it was strange to me. Oh—I'd seen Negroes before, but not like that. I'd never been expected to live with them. They were separate, something apart. They live around you but they're expected to be invisible, because it's more comfortable that way—and then something like the Army happens to you—and someone like George can never be invisible again. I remember that thing in the restaurant. We weren't exactly buddies—but after all we were in the same barracks. I'd tried to make up for that first day and George had been decent about it. Anyway we were in town and this restaurant thing happened. It was terrible.

NARRATOR: Repeat it for us.

PAUL: Why repeat ugliness?

NARRATOR: Even the ugly may have something to teach us. Repeat it—please.

> (*Light restaurant area in background where* GEORGE *is sitting at a table for two.* MAN *in apron standing behind counter to left.* PAUL, *turning reluctantly, walks past* COUNTERMAN *to table where* GEORGE *waits. As he passes* COUNTERMAN, *he turns in response to his call.*)

COUNTERMAN: Hey, Buddy.

PAUL: Yeah.

COUNTERMAN: I know they make you live with them on the base but that's your problem, not mine. I don't want him in my place. Get him out of here.

PAUL: Now just a minute. He's a friend of mine and—

COUNTERMAN: Like I said, soldier, you make friends with anybody you want but get him out of here now—peaceful like.

PAUL: Peaceful like. You're sure not acting very peaceful.

COUNTERMAN: Look, as long as I run this place I'll serve who I want and when I want. Now if you and your buddy give me any more trouble you're gonna regret it.

GEORGE *(Rising):* I'm not hungry, Paul. Let's go. Honest. I couldn't eat a thing. *(He walks off to right and meets the* NARRATOR *as the lights cross-fade from the restuarant to this limbo area.)* I meant it. I wasn't hungry any more. Things like that happen now and again. But you never really get used to it. When you do, you've lost a little bit of what makes a man tick, I think. But that's all over now—and one thing came out of it. I found a friend in Paul—a friend I still have.

NARRATOR: And now you're going to see him again—in his home town, a small Midwestern community—at his own school. You're going there on a scholarship, according to the letter Paul was reading. Do you expect your friendship to continue?

GEORGE: Why not? You sound like my grandfather. He had plenty to say when I left this morning. He's probably still saying it.

(Light GRANDFATHER *in limbo. As he speaks,* GEORGE *walks into his area to join dialogue.)*

GRANDFATHER: I am still saying it, George, and I'll be saying it to the day I die. It's no sin to tell somebody you love to be careful. It's not wrong to protect your children.

GEORGE: From what, Grandpa? What are you protecting me from? My friends—from Paul? You don't even know him. Do I need protection because my skin isn't white? Do I need protection from that school, Grandpa? That school that gave me a scholarship? Why can't I accept what's offered in the spirit in which it's offered? There's too much suspicion in the world, Grandpa, and I'm not going to live my life that way. I love you, but your way isn't mine.

GRANDFATHER: George, there's only one way for us—it's to remember we can be hurt. This isn't the Army, Boy. You're home now. And when you're home, you're supposed to keep your place. And if you've forgotten it, there'll be somebody to remind you where it is. That's what I'm trying to save you from.

GEORGE: Grandpa, my place is what I make it. No one can hurt me if I remember that. The days when we had a "place" to remember are over—and I'm not going to help them come back.

I'm not going where I'm not wanted because I'm not built that way. But I'm not going to stay out of places I have a right to be, and I'm certainly not going to stay away from places I'm asked to be—just out of fear. There isn't room for that kind of fear any more, Grandpa.

GRANDFATHER: There's always room for fear when there's something to be afraid of. This "welcome" you expect from your friend—boy—don't forget he has a family too. He has friends. How do you think they like the idea of your coming?

GEORGE: I don't know, Grandpa, I've thought about it. But they're Paul's family. Their feelings must be his feelings.

(*The area darkens. Light adjacent area where* PAUL *and* PAUL'S FATHER *are in discussion.*)

FATHER: Look, Son, you know how I feel about things like this. Now the Army is one thing—but you're home now and this boy just doesn't belong around here—not with our kind of people. I realize you promised to meet him when he comes in and you've got to be polite. But there are ways of making him understand that it can't be the way it was in the Army. After all—what can you two have in common?

PAUL: We have everything in common—everything except the color of our skins. We're both prelaw. We like the same kind of music. We agree on a lot of things—from baseball to the way we eat our hamburgers. But none of those things is really important. The important thing is that we like each other—and I'm not snubbing any friend of mine to satisfy "our kind of people."

FATHER: I can't stop you from making a fool of yourself, Son. I can only warn you—don't get involved in a crusade. Your friend's liable to get hurt—you're liable to get hurt, and Phyllis too. Are you asking her to buck the whole town?

(*The light in the area dims as the* NARRATOR *is spotlighted.*)

NARRATOR: And so—two friends are to meet—in circumstances destined to test the strength of the bonds between them—and the strength of the beliefs they hold in common—beliefs about the way men should live together. It was in the waiting room of the bus depot that the reunion took place. (*The area is lighted.* GEORGE *sits waiting. As the* NARRATOR *speaks,* PAUL *and* PHYLLIS *enter and his spot goes out.*) George, remember the bench where you waited for your friends? Now, Phyllis and Paul enter the scene and we have a reunion.

PAUL *(Embracing* GEORGE *as* PHYLLIS *stands by):* It's been a long time, man. I thought this day would never come.

GEORGE: You can blame it on the scholarship committee. They take their time about giving any of that education away for nothing. (*Turning to* PHYLLIS) You're Phyllis. I'd know you anywhere.

PHYLLIS: Hello, George. It's good to meet you. But how did you know me?

GEORGE: Soldiers have a way of talking about the people who are important to them.

PHYLLIS: Well, that's nice to hear. Paul must have a poetic side he's managed to keep secret. (*They laugh.*) Where are you staying, George?

GEORGE: Well—I've rented a room on Prospect Street. Mrs. Bailey's—that is, temporarily—until classes begin. Then I'll move onto the campus. I can't wait to have a look at it.

PAUL: Look, George, you have time for that. Let's get you settled in your room. Then you join Phyllis and me for dinner at the Inn. And later in the evening we'll show you the whole town including the campus—if you'd like to see it in the dark, that is.

GEORGE *(laughing):* Well—that sounds pretty good to me—if it—

PHYLLIS: Paul! I don't want to put a damper on this. But haven't you forgotten something?

PAUL: What's that, hon?

PHYLLIS: Your mother asked my parents over for dinner at your house tonight—and we're expected to be there. I'm sure George will understand.

PAUL: Oh, that's not so important. There's no reason why—

GEORGE: Now look. Don't be silly, Phyllis is right. Your folks expect you for dinner. You be there. I'm dog tired anyway and as soon as I settle in, I'm going to hit the sack.

PAUL: George—I'm sorry about this. It slipped my mind. I'll tell you what we'll do. You get a night's rest and tomorrow morning Phyllis and I'll pick you up for church. And after that we'll show you the town. Right, Phyllis?

PHYLLIS: Oh! Yes. George, that'll be fine. We'll take you to our church tomorrow.

GEORGE: Listen, I don't want to trouble you. It was nice enough of you to come down to meet me this way. Why don't we let it go until Monday when classes begin and I'll see you then?

PAUL: Church won't hurt you a bit. We'll pick you up in the morning. Understand?

GEORGE: Okay—okay. If you're sure you don't mind.

PHYLLIS: Of course not. Tomorrow morning for church.

(The area lights dim out.)

NARRATOR *(In limbo):* A shadow of awkwardness falls over the friendship of the two young men, an awkwardness brought about by a change in the setting, by a need to re-establish an old bond in what could be hostile surroundings. *(Turns)* Phyllis—do you welcome George with all your heart?

(A light falls on PHYLLIS *revealing her standing with a hat and prayer book.)*

PHYLLIS: How can I? He's a stranger to me. I—I'm not sure he belongs here. I don't think he belongs in our church—no matter what Paul says. It's going to be embarrassing.

NARRATOR: Why will it be embarrassing to have George worship with you? Is God's church restricted?

PHYLLIS: Oh, no. Please. It's not that. What kind of a person do you think I am? It's just that I know how people feel—my parents—Paul's parents—and so many others. I know how they feel and I don't want any trouble. Not for Paul, not for me— and not for George.

(PAUL suddenly appears at PHYLLIS' *side.)*

PAUL: Sometimes trouble can't be avoided. Sometimes it's important that you don't run away . . .

(Their spots go out, leaving only the NARRATOR.*)*

NARRATOR: And so—even an invitation to common worship can be a challenge if prejudice and ignorance prevail. But what are the consequences of a situation like this? There are many.

(Light PAUL'S FATHER *talking into phone as the* NARRATOR *disappears.)*

FATHER: Of course not. What do you think I am? Some kind of crackpot? I don't know where he gets his notions and I resent your thinking that I share them. No—I never heard of such a thing and you can bet your bottom dollar he'll hear about it from me. None of them, I don't care how educated, are going to join my church. Yes. Yes. Yes. You can tell them all to stop worrying. I'll talk to the boy. Oh—wait a minute—he's coming in now. I'll call you later, Harry. *(Hangs up.)*

PAUL: Hi, Dad.

FATHER: Paul, I've tried to be patient with you but you've gone too far. What are you trying to do to me?

PAUL: What are you talking about, anyway?

FATHER: You know what I'm talking about. I'm talking about your new friend. I'm talking about the way you foisted him off on our church yesterday. I'm talking about the way your mother and I felt when we saw you walk down the aisle with him and Phyllis. And how do you think her parents felt?

PAUL: Now wait a minute—

FATHER: It's about time you waited before you tried to turn the whole world upside down. They tell me that you've actually asked that boy to join the church—and that he's had the nerve to accept. It's not bad enough for one Sunday. No—that's not enough for my son. You want him around all the time. Pretty soon there'll be another and then another—and before you know it there won't be any room for us in our own church. Why can't you leave well enough alone? Why do you have to start all this trouble? How plain does it have to be made that your friend isn't welcome here?

PAUL: I don't understand you. I really don't, Dad. A man looks different from you and you make an enemy of him. You don't want to see him, you don't want to talk to him, you want to blot him out. You don't even know George. You've made it so that I can't bring one of my friends to my own house.

FATHER: These things have to be taken slowly. I know the world's changing. But you can't do everything at once. It's a simple matter of people staying where they belong—and you —you were never like this. You didn't have anything to do with them. What did they do to you in the Army, anyway?

PAUL: Nobody did anything to me, Dad. It was a simple matter of learning from experience that a man is a man no matter what he looks like. I learned that from being with all kinds of people and it's something I don't want to forget. I don't understand why you want to cut yourself off from half the human race. And I certainly would like to know where you and your friends get the authority to bar a man from church. I've always been under the impression that a church was one place where everyone is welcome.

FATHER: There's room enough for them in their own churches. Why make us uncomfortable in ours?

(*The lights cross-fade to the* NARRATOR.)

NARRATOR (*In limbo*): One word out of this whole unpleasantness provides us with a clue to the conflict. The word, used by Paul's father, was "uncomfortable." And discomfort brings out irritability—misunderstanding. (*Turns*) Phyllis—are you uncomfortable with George?

(*The lights go up on* PHYLLIS.)

PHYLLIS: I don't know—I just don't know any more. I mean anyone has a right to go to church. And George is a decent boy. Paul is crazy about him. But I still feel that people have the right here to live their own lives the way they want to live them. Is it necessary for a perfectly nice boy to upset everyone like this?

(*Suddenly* PAUL *joins her.*)

PAUL: The minister isn't upset.

PHYLLIS: The minister? Oh, Paul—how did you bring him into it?

PAUL: He's the minister, isn't he, Phyllis? He didn't have to be brought in. This is something that is important to him. He told me that as long as George is going to school here, he'll be more than welcome as a member of the congregation.

PHYLLIS: And what about the others—the people who live here— who belong here? Don't they count for anything? What's Dr. Craig going to do about them? They won't stand still for it. Is he going to defy everyone?

PAUL: I guess that's one way of putting it.

PHYLLIS: Oh—sometimes you're so smug. Suppose this thing costs Dr. Craig his job. How will you feel about your "crusade" then?

PAUL: Listen to me, Phyllis. I didn't start this thing as a "crusade." I simply asked a friend of mine to join my church. Everyone has made a big thing out of what started as an ordinary act of courtesy. As far as Dr. Craig is concerned—his job, I mean—he knows the risks but for him it's a matter of integrity—his Christian faith—and if he didn't have that he wouldn't be any good as a minister anyway.

PHYLLIS: Paul, you're too much for me. It's all too much for me. I don't know what's right or what's wrong any more. I only know one thing. (GEORGE *enters to rear here.*) I'm sorry I ever heard of George. He's caused nothing but trouble ever since he came and I'm sick of it. Why couldn't he stay where he belonged? Why didn't he go to church where he could be comfortable—where there wouldn't have been all this fighting? I've tried to understand. I've tried to like him. But how can you like someone when he does nothing but irritate all your friends, all of the people who mean anything to you? Why doesn't he go back where he belongs?

GEORGE: Phyllis—I don't know what to say to you except that I'm sorry. I made a mistake, I guess. I thought of Paul as my friend and I guess I took it for granted that everyone else would be. I should have known better. I've been told often enough to be careful of my place. But I forgot, I guess. I thought my grandfather was talking about something dead and buried. Now I can see—some things never change.

PHYLLIS: George—I'm sorry. I didn't know you were there. I never would have—

GEORGE: What's the difference whether I was there or not? What is important is the way you feel about me—and I heard the truth about that. I guess the only way you hear the truth is to sneak up on it—surprise it. And, then, sometimes, it surprises you.

PAUL: George, we want you with us. Dr. Craig wants you. Phyllis is upset. She—

GEORGE: She's upset. What about me? What about us? Aren't we supposed to get upset? Paul—I know you want to be my friend. But let's face it. It wasn't meant to be. I'm not blaming anybody. That's just the way it is. I can tell you both I've never pushed in where I wasn't wanted and I'm not beginning now. Don't worry, Phyllis. You can go back to being comfortable. I'm sorry for the trouble I caused you. I'll see you both—around. (*He exits.*)

PHYLLIS: Paul—what have I done?

PAUL: It's not you alone, Phyllis. We've all done it to him—and we've done it to ourselves.

(*The lights dim on* PAUL *and* PHYLLIS *and come up on the* NARRATOR.)

NARRATOR: This may well be the important sin. The sin we commit against ourselves—not by design but by failure to recognize the God-given equality of every man—and the reluctance to accept God-given differences between men, differences implying not inferiority but a divine variety. Every action, every sin is the action, the sin of an individual—and there is another sin, the sin of pride. It can operate in any man—no matter what his faith, no matter what his color. George—

(*A light appears on* GEORGE.)

GEORGE: What do you want with me?

NARRATOR: I'd like you to talk with your grandfather.

GEORGE: I should talk with my grandfather. He knows what the world is. Age gives a man the kind of knowledge he needs to live a life without hurt.

GRANDFATHER (*Lit beside* GEORGE *as the spot goes out on the* NARRATOR): You can't live a life without hurt, George. That isn't what I was trying to tell you. The hurt will come from a thousand different places in a thousand unexpected ways. But, boy, you left yourself open to it. You didn't protect yourself. And when something like this happens to you, it nearly kills you inside. It takes a long time getting over something like that. And that's why I tried to protect you. As long as you play the game according to the rules, you'll be able to take whatever they hand out.

GEORGE: Whose rules? Theirs? What kind of rules are they?

GRANDFATHER: You know what kind they are. All I'm telling you is that you have no choice. Keep your place and you won't be bothered.

GEORGE: That's the trouble. I really have no place—unless I believe what you tell me and go back instead of forward.

GRANDFATHER: Call it back—call it forward—call it what you want, boy. Your fingers have been burnt. Are you going to burn them again?

GEORGE: No. I'm not going to burn them again. I tried and I'm not really sorry I did. But I was wrong and you were right. Some things never change. It's their game and I'll play by their rules.

(GEORGE *picks up his suitcase and the lights come up on the bus terminal area, fading simultaneously on the* GRANDFATHER. PAUL *enters the area.*)

PAUL: George.

GEORGE: Yeah.

PAUL: Where are you going?

GEORGE: Home.

PAUL: Home?

GEORGE: Yeah. I have a home. It's a place where people look at me and like me—a place where I'm wanted, where I can go to church.

PAUL: George—if you want me to, I'll say I'm sorry. But you ought to know it without my saying a word.

GEORGE: That's a big help.

PAUL: I don't get you, George. You're no child. You must have been running into this your whole life.

GEORGE: That doesn't mean I have to like it—or take it. Your high and mighty friends—your high and mighty Christian friends.

PAUL: Let's leave them out of it. Just for a minute—let's leave them out of it. Let's talk about you and me. What have I done to make you angry with me? Did I create this thing? Have I helped it along?

GEORGE: Yeah, you've helped it along a great deal. You want to know how? By bringing me here to show off with. By making a monkey of me in front of your friends and in front of myself. By getting to me so that I let my guard down for just a second too long. By making me believe that we were friends—and that for once, just once, there was no color bar between two guys who liked each other. That's how you helped it along, Buddy. Because it wasn't true. None of it was true—and I should have known it from the beginning.

PAUL: I asked you to come to my church because you were a friend of mine. If you want to believe it was some kind of trick, I can't stop you. But you're tricking yourself. You won't

give anybody a chance. You've been hurt and you're mad at
the world. I know as well as you do that what you've heard
and what I've seen are ugly and rotten. I've lived with that
poison in my own home. That doesn't mean I like it or that
I'm going to stop fighting it. But how can I—if people like
you pull back the minute you get hurt in a fight?

GEORGE: Who are you to talk to me? What do you know about
it? You're white, you're blond, you have the proper religious
background. No one's door has ever shut in your face—and
there are some names you can never be called. (*Pause.*)
You've got the most colossal nerve I've ever seen—to judge
me, accuse me for your sins and the sins of your father and
his father, too.

PAUL: I know I haven't gone through the things you have,
George. But I've had my own share of trouble in learning how
to live. George, sit down. This may not be the way to per-
suade you to stay here and stick it out, but I'm going to tell
you the truth, anyway. George, the first time I laid eyes on
you, I didn't want you around. You know why? Because
you were a Negro, because I didn't want to live with a Negro
—a stranger.

GEORGE: It figures. I was right to begin with. You're a hypo-
crite. (*He turns away.*)

PAUL (*Holding him*): No, listen to me, please. I learned something. You taught me something just by being there, by being
yourself. You taught me something. You're no stranger to
me now, George. You're a man who is important to me.
What I'm trying to tell you is that I learned something from
you I never had an opportunity to know before. How could
I? Look at this town. There are no Negroes here, or there
are so few it amounts to the same thing. And—unfortunately,
people are afraid of the things they don't know, don't understand. I had to fight a battle with myself when I first met you.
All the false, rotten lies that I had accepted without question—
all the fears that build up around the unknown—all of them
had to go out the window just because I met you. What I'm
asking you to do is to help these other people the way you
helped me. Show them how wrong they are.

GEORGE: Why should I? What do you think I am—a guinea pig?

PAUL: No—I think you're a man, and I'm asking you to play a man's role. I'm asking you to help Dr. Craig show them to themselves. Believe me, I know I'm asking a lot. I'm not sure I could do it. But you owe it to yourself to try.

GEORGE: You don't know what you want from me. How can I go into that church every Sunday morning knowing that most of the people don't want me around?

PAUL: I don't know how you can do it. That's a burden you have to bear for yourself. But I'm asking you to try because— sooner or later—the people you're talking about will become fewer and fewer.

GEORGE: Oh, that's fine. You mean if I keep coming back for more eventually they'll get to tolerate me.

PAUL: That's right, George—because even tolerance is a beginning.

GEORGE: You're asking too much. You're asking something from me that I'm not sure I can give—and I think you're asking something of yourself that you'd better think about twice. Are you sure you can take it? Are you sure you're willing to stand up to the people you've lived with all your life—people who won't like your friendship for me? You've got to be honest with me. Are you sure, Paul—are you sure?

PAUL: I'm sure I'll try. I can tell you that.

GEORGE: Do you think you have the right to ask me to do this just because you're going to "try"? Do you have it? Paul? Do you have the right to ask me to expose myself like that?

PAUL: I don't know, George. I just don't know.

(*The lights dim on the bus terminal area as the* NARRATOR *is spotlighted.*)

NARRATOR: The question of man's relation to man is a part of the infinitely greater question of man's relation to God. The seeking years—the growing years—are questioning years—and the questions that young men and women ask are a part of growing up. "No man is an island entire of itself; every man is a piece of the continent, a part of the main—any man's death diminishes me because I am involved in mankind, and therefore never send to know for whom the bell tolls; it tolls for thee."

Curtain

PRODUCTION NOTES

The Set In staging this play on television, one particular device added greatly to its effectiveness. The device, which came to be referred to as a "jury box," consisted of two platforms a step difference in height, the higher placed directly behind the lower. There was a railing across the back, another across the front, and a rail splitting the unit into two areas. At the back of one area were seated Paul's father and his fiancée, Phyllis; at the front of it Paul, on the lower step. At the back of the other side was George's grandfather, and in front George. All the entrances and exits were made from and to this "jury box."

It will be immediately apparent that the rail down the middle symbolizes the social separation between the two races involved in the story, and that the jury box itself carries the feeling of being an island. There is every reason to believe that this device would be equally effective on stage, and these notes are written with it in mind. The jury box should be placed directly upstage center. Down center is a limbo area. Here the phone scene may be played. Down right is the Army barracks, which can be suggested by as simple a dressing as two Army cots. Down left is the waiting room, consisting of a bench, perhaps a bulletin board of arrivals and departures, or a baggage counter. Upstage left of center is the restaurant, consisting of a table with two chairs and a counter. Coffee urns, more chairs, etc., may be added as space and facilities permit. Note that the three areas with set pieces should be struck and set.

In the matter of lighting it has been suggested that a strong effect may be gained by lighting the jury box throughout the performance, dimming it whenever another scene is being played.

Costumes Paul and George have a change from civvies to Army clothes and back. Time does not permit a complete change, so this must be kept simple. It will probably prove enough for them to take off the jackets they wear at the opening of the play, tuck their ties into their shirts in Army fashion and put on fatigue caps. Paul's father, George's grandfather, and Phyllis wear appropriate street clothes, and the counterman a shirt and long apron.

Props Letter, book, duffle bag, shoebrush and cloth, suitcase, and phone.

THE FAITH
HAWKER

By Howard Rodman

originally broadcast
July 28, 1957

The cast:

THE HAWKER_____.Dort Clark

DONALD_____Fritz Weber

ALEXANDRA_____.Patricia Bosworth

MARCELLA_____.Sybil White

NARRATOR_____.Donald Symington

DIRECTED BY_____James MacAllen

SCENE

As the curtain rises, we see, down right, THE HAWKER *in back of his fold-away, velvet-covered stand, on which is displayed a row of medicine bottles filled with a clear liquid.* THE HAWKER *is a man who looks like Walter Huston, shirt sleeves rolled up, a jaunty straw hat, and a Coney Island barker's cane slung over one wrist.*

THE HAWKER: Now step up, Ladies and Gentlemen! Now step up! Step up close as you like and look as long as you like! Now I want you all to gather around and take a good look at what I have for you here! (*He raises bottle on high.*) I want you to notice that the liquid in this bottle looks like water, smells like water, and tastes like water, if you taste it! But this colorless, odorless, tasteless liquid is one of the great miracles of the age! Because if you drink it, and there is anything wrong with you; mind you, I said ANYTHING, then this liquid, this miracle, will cure and will remedy all the known and unknown ailments, traumas, diseases, illnesses, injuries, afflictions, and problems of man and woman! This is the universal panacea that all the learned men of the most important countries of the world have been searching for since the beginning of time! Step right up and take a bottle for yourself, absolutely free! That's right, I said free! I have drunk of this stuff and I am now incapable of making a profit on the misery of others! Step up and take a bottle for yourself!

(*He holds a bottle triumphantly aloft, then stops his spiel as he sees that he is still alone. He laughs a dry little laugh to himself, shrugs, and puts the bottle down. He takes time out to light a cigarette with a match he scratches alive on the sole of his shoe. The* NARRATOR *enters the stage and crosses to the fold-away stand.*)

111

NARRATOR: Good morning, sir.

THE HAWKER: Good morning, sir.

NARRATOR: I've been listening to you.

THE HAWKER: Then I'm one up for the day. Most of the time I spend talking to myself.

(*The* NARRATOR *reaches for one of the bottles.*)

NARRATOR: May I—?

THE HAWKER: Help yourself. (*The* NARRATOR *takes a bottle, examines it, unscrews the top, smells it, pours a little onto a finger and tastes it.*) I give you my word, it's as pure as water. As a matter of fact, I give you my word it is nothing but water. Help yourself; particularly if you're thirsty.

NARRATOR: Certainly you wouldn't waste your time just giving water away?

THE HAWKER: I used to give away empty bottles; but then I discovered that man is a funny animal: he doesn't want what he can't see, feel, smell, hear, and taste. So I put water into the bottles.

NARRATOR: And that's how you make your living?

THE HAWKER: I don't sell these, Mister; I give them away.

NARRATOR: Why?

THE HAWKER (*Studies the* NARRATOR): What do you do?

NARRATOR: I'm a student. I study philosophy.

THE HAWKER: I finished studying a long time ago; I practice philosophy. I belong to an old and well-ordered, and sometimes respected, profession. My friend, I'm a faith healer. But before you get me wrong, let me hasten to inform you that what that means is that I heal faith.

NARRATOR: With water?

THE HAWKER: I told you before, the content of the bottle doesn't matter. It works as well when the bottles are empty. (*He smiles.*) That is the nature of faith.

NARRATOR: To believe there's something in the bottle when there isn't?

THE HAWKER: Simply to believe! Have a bottle; it's on the house.

NARRATOR: Thank you.

THE HAWKER: All right, Ladies and Gentlemen, step right up! Come a little closer so you can hear what I say . . .

(THE HAWKER's *voice fades away as the lights follow the* NARRATOR *who crosses away from* THE HAWKER *into limbo, stopping to think about the bottle in his hand. The* NARRATOR *speaks directly to the audience.*)

NARRATOR: We shall see more of this man. A thread of his life leads directly to the college in which I study, and is intertwined with the threads of other lives. The nature of the question this man raises will be examined: What is faith? Does it have a shape, a texture, a tangible form? Can it be encompassed in a bottle? Like this one (*he holds up the bottle*)— or this one?

(*The lights dissolve to the restaurant area. There is a table covered with a checkered tablecloth; two glasses on the table, and a beer bottle.* ALEXANDRA *and* DONALD *are sitting at the table. They are not looking at each other though they sit side by side. The girl is tracing abstract designs on the tablecloth with her fingernail; the boy is staring into his glass.*)

NARRATOR: The name of this girl is Alexandra Drake. She's a junior, and her marks are in the upper half of her class. This boy's name is Donald Alsh, and he is a senior. His marks are spotty. Excellent marks for the subjects he prefers; bad marks in those subjects which do not seem to interest him. This boy and this girl have known each other now for some three years. In a vague and general way without any definite stipulation, they've considered themselves engaged. But now, it seems, they will not be married. Because Donald doesn't believe in marriage.

ALEXANDRA: You don't have to be angry at me. I'm trying to understand.

DONALD: I'm not angry.

ALEXANDRA: You must have been thinking about this for a long time.

DONALD (*Nods*): I didn't have the guts to say it before.

ALEXANDRA: We've been going together for three years.

DONALD: That doesn't give you a hold on me!

ALEXANDRA: I was just thinking how strange it is that we evaded the subject for three years straight.

DONALD: I guess.

ALEXANDRA: Never spoke of marriage, or children, or a home. Never mentioned what we'd do when college was done.

DONALD: We had fun.

ALEXANDRA: No complaints.

DONALD: Not any expressed complaints, anyhow.

ALEXANDRA: I'm not going to let you pick a fight with me. That's too easy.

DONALD: I don't want any fights.

ALEXANDRA (Finally): I don't suppose you'd care to tell me why.

DONALD: Why! The whole world is why. Look around you. Here a cold war, there a cold war. Do you think I'm going to bring kids into that? I go into the Army, and I come out and then what? Do you want to wait while I'm in the Army? Or do you want to follow me from post to post?

ALEXANDRA: I don't believe those reasons.

DONALD: No, you'd like to oversimplify the whole thing! You'd like to turn it into a simple little boy-girl equation: boy is tired of girl, ergo, hence, boy will not marry girl. For the record, I'm not tired of you. For the record, I grow more in love with you every day. I'm not going to spoil your life, that's all. There's nothing to depend on, there's nothing you can count on, there's nothing ahead.

ALEXANDRA: And if we don't see each other any more, does that make it better or worse?

DONALD: Neither. It just fits in with the pattern of the way things are.

ALEXANDRA: Why, now?

DONALD: I kept putting it off, because I'm pretty much of a coward. How much longer can I stall? I'll be graduated in another month. I'm not that lousy: to put it off until graduation day without a word.

ALEXANDRA: I don't want to cry here, in front of you, and in public, Donald; so I'm going to leave in a minute. Just listen to me for that minute, though. I know that this is my own fault; a lot of it is my own fault—please don't say anything until I'm finished—it's my own fault because this isn't the first time you've been so pessimistic about everything, and this isn't the first time you've hidden yourself from me. Just that I didn't understand how deep it went, that's all. I thought as time went on you'd grow out of it. That's really my own problem. What I want to say, Donald, is that I'm hurt. Just for one reason. Because I thought that when two people are in love, then they have each other to depend on, and they can count on each other. The thing that hurts is that you don't trust me. And the thing that hurts is that I love you and I'm not enough to make you secure with my love. That's all. Good-bye, Donald.

(*She rises and holds out her hand for him to shake. He pretends not to see it, and* ALEXANDRA *leaves. The* NARRATOR *enters the picture and sits down at the table. He waits for* DONALD *to speak first.*)

DONALD (*Finally*): "Each man kills the thing he loves: the coward does it with a kiss, the brave man with a sword."

NARRATOR: And after that?

DONALD: After the crime, the punishment. To go alone in the world, cut off from every human being: that's the punishment.

NARRATOR: Self-imposed?

DONALD: Each man his own criminal, his own judge and jury, in this do-it-yourself of all worlds! Economy and efficiency to the nth degree!

NARRATOR: But to be a judge and jury, a man has to have trust in himself—

DONALD: No trust! The verdict will be unfair!

NARRATOR: One must believe in something.

DONALD: Not I! Shall I say I believe in myself? No. For I am a self-confessed murderer of the thing I love. Who can trust a murderer? Not I! I have no faith in myself. I'll tell you a secret. I have no faith in anything. The world falls apart every day into smaller and smaller particles, diminishing faith into smaller and smaller particles! (*Takes the* NARRATOR's *wrist, and forces the* NARRATOR's *palm to rest flat on the table.*) Is this a table under my hand? It is not a table! It is a collection of vagrant atoms! And what is an atom? A nucleus and a series of electrons! And what are electrons? Energy. And what is the difference between energy and matter? There is none—they are interchangeable! What is the nature of energy? Who knows? And that is what is the matter with matter—that no one knows the matter of energy! And therefore no one knows anything! And if you say you know, you lie!

NARRATOR: You're playing with words. A table is a table. And truth is truth. Just as right is right, and wrong is wrong.

DONALD: Oh, you believe! One is one, and the rest is simple for you! One is one. Let me give you my philosophy: one is not one. One is zero. The world is nothing; life is nothing. I take that back, life is something. To be born is a crime, and life is the punishment. And everything else is uncertain.

NARRATOR: The sun will rise in the East tomorrow morning!

DONALD: It may. And if it does, you will say that there is the proof of your statement. But that's no proof until after the fact. It may rise tomorrow. If it does, then I can say it has risen. Until then, nothing is certain. And you may look at me and say I'm drunk, but I'm not drunk. I don't like to drink. Here's my glass. I poured myself half a glass and that's what's left. I'm not drunk: I'm sick to my stomach with fear, because the only thing I can believe in are the days I've already lived; the minutes that are already past. And I don't know what the next minute brings!

(*The* NARRATOR *sits a moment longer before moving. Then as the lights fade on the restaurant scene, he moves away speaking to the audience.*)

NARRATOR: It often happens that young lovers quarrel, and feel sorry for themselves, and behave extravagantly, and talk wildly. But this goes deeper; this is a young man without faith in anything. The question rises, can a human being live without faith? We shall see.

(*His stroll takes him to* THE HAWKER's *area.* THE HAWKER *is doing nothing, seated, waiting.*)

NARRATOR: Still here?

THE HAWKER: I'm waiting.

NARRATOR: For someone special?

THE HAWKER: I'm waiting for someone who needs faith.

NARRATOR: How do you know they'll come?

THE HAWKER: Not they. Just one person.

NARRATOR: How do you know?

THE HAWKER: The magnet draws the compass point. The sun draws the birds, north and south, and north again. The flower leans toward the light, and those who are ill will search round the world for a remedy. Let me ask you, son: Isn't a man without faith a sick man?

NARRATOR: Yes, he is.

(THE HAWKER *tips his hand to the* NARRATOR, *and the* NARRATOR *nods and passes on. The lights stay on the* NARRATOR *and fade on* THE HAWKER'S *area. The* NARRATOR *speaks as he walks.*)

NARRATOR: One more person we must meet: Alexandra's roommate, Marcella Baker. (*Gestures to the lighting man*) The park bench, please.

(*The light comes up on the bench, revealing* DONALD *and* MARCELLA.)

NARRATOR: That's Marcella. When Alexandra came home and threw herself on the bed, and cried, and could hardly speak out what was wrong, Marcella went out to find Donald. And she told him.

MARCELLA: Don't you care?

DONALD: No. I don't have any feelings.

MARCELLA: You're hurting her.

DONALD: She'll get over me.

MARCELLA: She won't. Don't you understand anything? Why do you think she never spoke about marriage to you? She took it on faith! She took you on faith!

DONALD: Evidently she was wrong.

MARCELLA: I don't believe you!

DONALD: Drop it. (*Finally*) I'm doing exactly what I think is right to do. Let her cry now and not later. Let her cry now, untouched by me, and later she'll be free to meet somebody else, to love somebody else. I have nothing to give her. I have nothing to give anybody!

MARCELLA: Then don't give. Just take. Just take what she has to give you. Don't shut her off!

DONALD: How long can somebody give and give and get nothing in return without killing you for it!

MARCELLA: This is not a jungle! This is not a world where people kill like animals.

DONALD: Isn't it! Pick up your newspapers, and find any page; count them—the people driven mad by anguish and despair; killing their children, their husbands, their wives, themselves! Pick up a newspaper and read about a bomb dropped on a city of three hundred thousand in 1945—men, women, and children! Use your eyes, don't blind yourself! And what happens to these poor, helpless, miserable wretches who kill? We hunt them down and we kill them! The world is full of the deaths of human beings murdered by other human beings! And don't tell me this isn't so! Don't lie to me, and make me lie to myself! Do you want a jungle? I give you the minds and the hearts of human beings!

MARCELLA: Maybe it's like that, Donald. But we hate it to be like that. More and more we try not to be like that. Don't we, Donald?

DONALD: Go away, Marcella, before I destroy every last belief you have. I warn you, go away!

MARCELLA: If the world is full of tragedy, is that any excuse for making Alexandra's life a tragedy?

DONALD: Go away, Marcella! Marcella, I don't want the company of other people! I need to be by myself, alone, whatever it costs!

MARCELLA: It doesn't matter, Donald, if you drive me away. But don't do that to Alexandra, is all I'm saying. Don't you see? She loves you; and if you dry that up, then don't you see, she doesn't have anything to fall back on, either.

(DONALD *deliberately and rudely turns his back.* MARCELLA *can think of nothing more to say, no further appeal to make. She leaves. After a while,* DONALD *rises and shoves his hands deep into his pockets, and walks away through limbo to where* THE HAWKER *waits.*)

THE HAWKER: Greetings! *(But* DONALD *ignores him, tries to pass on as if he had neither seen nor heard the man. This* THE HAWKER *will not allow. He stands between* DONALD *and his path.)* I have something for you. *(He takes* DONALD's *arm in a firm grip, takes a bottle from the fold-away tray and displays it to* DONALD.*)* Here! The panacea of the ages! The sovereign remedy for all the ills of man; body and soul.

DONALD: Will it cure being alive?

THE HAWKER: It will make it more palatable to be alive.

DONALD: Alive, without suffering?

THE HAWKER: Without suffering.

DONALD: That's a cheat: it's robbing Peter to pay Paul.
(He starts on again and again THE HAWKER *catches his arm and holds him back.)*

THE HAWKER: Explain that to me; I didn't follow you.

DONALD: To be alive without suffering is to be swallowed up in guilt. To live in a world so rotten, so corrupt as this, and not feel shame? How could one live with the guilt of not being ashamed?

THE HAWKER: Take the bumblebee who goes to the flower and takes what's sweet! Is he ashamed?

DONALD: I wish I had the conscience of a bumblebee!

THE HAWKER: It's not a matter of conscience. It's a matter of faith. The bumblebee believes. He believes that all is well and fitting, and he does his job because that's the way he's made.

DONALD: And the way I'm made, I ask questions. And I look for a truthful answer. And I'm not satisfied that being is its own excuse. And I've asked the question again and again: Why are we here? For what purpose? And I've met no one who could give me an answer. No one.
(THE HAWKER *holds up the bottle again.)*

THE HAWKER: Here's an answer. Drink this and see.

DONALD: Not interested.

THE HAWKER: Not interested! Not interested enough to find out the contents of a little bottle, and yet you ask the fundamental questions about existence! What do you think is in this bottle?

DONALD: I don't know.

THE HAWKER: Satisfy your curiosity. One quarter. Twenty-five cents. Maybe it's only water in here. Maybe if you give me the twenty-five cents, you're just throwing it away. On the other hand, I'm a stranger to you: what reason would I have for cheating you? Twenty-five cents; is it a bargain?

DONALD: No.

THE HAWKER: Son, you don't even have a quarter's worth of faith—you're dead.

DONALD: I may be.   I've often asked the question—am I alive?
(THE HAWKER *eyes* DONALD, *studying him.* DONALD *shrugs and walks away into darkness.* THE HAWKER *calls after him.*)

THE HAWKER: Son!   If not for a quarter, will you pay half a dollar?   Will you pay a dollar?   Five dollars?

DONALD: No.   No.
(DONALD *walks away.   The* NARRATOR *enters the picture, crossing to* THE HAWKER.   THE HAWKER *turns to the* NARRATOR.)

THE HAWKER: A strange boy.   I knew he didn't trust enough to take a gift for nothing.   I thought a nominal fee might subdue his suspicions a little.   I was wrong.   Then I raised the price, and raised it, and still he wouldn't take it from me.   A strange boy.

NARRATOR: Why should he pay for it when he wouldn't take it for nothing?

THE HAWKER: Many people are like that.   If they don't believe in anything else, at least they believe in money.   At least they trust the cost of things.   Isn't that one of the logics of the world: the more things cost, the more they're worth?

NARRATOR: Is he the one you were expecting?

THE HAWKER: Yes.

NARRATOR: What do you want from him?

THE HAWKER: I told you: I heal faith.

NARRATOR: With a cheat?   With water pretending to be a sovereign remedy?

THE HAWKER: Think of the good it would have done that boy to take me on face value.

NARRATOR: But you're trying to sell him a fake.

THE HAWKER: Well, then, after he found he was cheated, think of the good it would have done him to learn to forgive.   Think how much good it would do a boy like that to learn that though I cheated him there are others in the world who are honest!   And would it be a cheat?   I said I sell faith in a bottle!   Wouldn't he be getting faith if he trusted himself enough to take a bottle?

NARRATOR: Isn't that a game you're playing with words?

THE HAWKER: All words are toys: like numbers. Anyone can prove anything he wants to with words or numbers. Do I feel? That's the question!

NARRATOR: Who are you?

THE HAWKER: I'll answer that later. Do me the courtesy to allow me to answer in my own good time.

NARRATOR: You're still waiting, then?

THE HAWKER: Oh, yes. I must.

NARRATOR: How long will you wait now?

THE HAWKER: Some months. Some hundred days. Twenty-four hundred hours. A hundred forty-four thousand minutes—

(THE HAWKER *turns away as he begins the speech above, crossing back to his fold-away stand. As he reaches the stand, the light goes out on him, leaving the* NARRATOR *alone, and the voice of* THE HAWKER, *too, fades away, before he finishes the speech. The* NARRATOR *speaks directly to the audience.*)

NARRATOR: Time is strange: an hour may go by slowly while we clutch desperately to hold a fleeting year. And so some months do go by: for the man who sells faith, for Donald Alsh, and for Alexandra Drake. But one thing is sure as time passes: something happens. In the shortest time, or the longest, something happens. And in this time of a few months, Alexandra becomes sick. A deadly illness, even in these days of antibiotics. Meningitis.

(*He holds out his hand to gesture toward the area where* ALEXANDRA *is lying in a hospital bed. The lights go up on that area, excluding the* NARRATOR. *A few feet away* MARCELLA *bars the way to the bed to* DONALD, *who has a small bunch of flowers in his hand.*)

DONALD: Please let me see her.

MARCELLA: You can't.

DONALD: Please. No matter how you feel about me, let me see her.

MARCELLA: It isn't that, Donald. She can't see anyone. She has to be absolutely still.

DONALD: Is she very ill?

MARCELLA: Yes, she is.

DONALD: She's not going to die, is she?

MARCELLA: We don't know.

DONALD: Don't the doctors know? They can do anything to-day! They can do anything!

MARCELLA: They've tried everything they know. All they can do now is to pray. That's all anybody can do.

(DONALD *turns away. Then he turns back and hands the flowers to* MARCELLA. *She takes them without a word, and then lights fade on the hospital area and go up on* THE HAWKER. DONALD *crosses into this area, and he and* THE HAWKER *look at each other.*)

THE HAWKER: I knew you would come back.

DONALD: I have no place else to go. I need what you have.

THE HAWKER: There's a price on it.

DONALD: Whatever the price.

THE HAWKER: All the money you have, of course.

DONALD: That doesn't matter.

THE HAWKER: You're a strange boy. I expected you'd bargain more.

DONALD: No.

THE HAWKER: I have something special for you. (*Reaches down and brings up a bottle which is colored differently from the others.*) Do you notice? This one isn't the color of water. This is a lovely green, don't you think so?

DONALD: What's the difference between this one and the others?

THE HAWKER: There's the inquisitive mind for you. This one is colored green.

DONALD: Does that make it better?

THE HAWKER: Why, you're beginning to have faith in me. You'll take my word, won't you?

DONALD: Yes, I will. Someone I care for very much is very sick. The doctors can't do anything for her.

THE HAWKER: That's too bad. You think this might help her?

DONALD: I can't think of anything else.

THE HAWKER: Well, it might, and it might not.

DONALD: What do you mean?

THE HAWKER: It won't do her any harm, that's for sure.

DONALD: Don't tease me! What do you mean?

THE HAWKER: What I say: it just won't do her any harm.

DONALD: I don't like the way you're talking. What are you getting at?

THE HAWKER: The lesson!

DONALD: What lesson?

THE HAWKER: The one you have coming to you! You've got nothing to believe in, so you'll turn to nothing when you're in trouble!

DONALD: You said you could help!

THE HAWKER: I *said!*

DONALD: You said it was a sovereign remedy—

THE HAWKER: I lied.

DONALD: No, you didn't!

THE HAWKER: I lied.

DONALD: You said it was a panacea for all the ills of man!

THE HAWKER: I lied!

DONALD: Why? Why?

THE HAWKER: Well, it's a sovereign remedy for the ills of fools. It opens their eyes and smartens them up when they find they've been stung!

DONALD: I want a bottle!

THE HAWKER: It's just water, that's all!

DONALD: The green one!

THE HAWKER: That's just water and a little vegetable dye!

DONALD: I want it!

THE HAWKER: Oh, you think it'll help her!

DONALD: Give it to me!

THE HAWKER: I told you it's a fake!

DONALD: It can't be!

THE HAWKER: It's a fake.

(*He pours the contents of the bottle onto the ground.*)

DONALD: Why? Why did you do that?

THE HAWKER: Because it wouldn't have done you any good. That's why.

DONALD: You must have something that'll help!

THE HAWKER: No, nothing.

DONALD: There must be something!

THE HAWKER: Nothing! You know it! That's the way the world is: lies and cheats and frauds, stealers and robbers and swindlers and murderers. *(He snaps shut the fold-away tray.)*

DONALD: What am I going to do now? Where can I turn now? *(He crosses away from* THE HAWKER *to the bench. He sits down on it, numbed, rubbing the wood on the bench.)* Wood isn't wood. It's moving atoms made up of electrons vanishing into energy made up of nothing. I pray you, make her well!

THE HAWKER: Might as well pray to me as pray to that! What's that: moving atoms! Nothing!

DONALD: There's got to be something!

THE HAWKER: What could there be? It's all nothing.

DONALD: No! Something holds it all together! Something gives it shape and purpose! Something moved those atoms here into a piece of wood. *(Hits himself.)* And something arranged me as a living thing! Something!

THE HAWKER: What? I ask you, boy! What could there be?

DONALD: I don't know! But something!

THE HAWKER: All the wise men sitting together and they couldn't answer that question, and you know.

DONALD: I don't know! I feel it! I believe it! It must be so. *(He kneels.)* I do not know your shape. I do not know what You are. I do not know if you can hear me. And if you can, I do not know if you want to listen! But please, please let her live; let her live. If I must die in her place, then let me die. But let her live. Let her live.

(His head droops onto his chest, and he cries. THE HAWKER *takes out a handkerchief, and dries his own eyes. The* NARRATOR *enters the picture, crossing to* THE HAWKER.)

NARRATOR: Is this the time? Will you tell me who you are now?

THE HAWKER *(Points):* That boy. The way he would have turned out: mocking, sneering, believing in nothing. Cheated, and fooled, and rotting slowly away. That's who I am.

NARRATOR: And now, as time goes by, you mean, he's going to turn into you?

THE HAWKER: Oh, no. Not now. Look at him. Don't you see what he did? He took off his gown of arrogance. He settled for not knowing everything. He settled for not being all-powerful. He let himself be touched by need. He let himself feel for somebody else. He laid himself open to the terrors of loving, loving when you might lose what you love. He said there's something bigger than he is. Do you think a man like that could turn into a fraud like me?

(He shakes his head, and slowly walks away. The NARRATOR *speaks directly to the audience.)*

NARRATOR: Time passes, and time heals. Alexandra is well. Perhaps through prayer, perhaps not. We do not know the ways of God.

(The lights rise to reveal ALEXANDRA *and* DONALD *talking quietly together on a bench.)*

NARRATOR: The world is not changed very much. But it is a little by the addition of the faith of even one man. Without faith we quit and give up, and life *is* a punishment for being born. And faith is the great gift: to believe is the only door which opens on a future free of dread.

Curtain

PRODUCTION NOTES

Mood This story deals with a search, a search for faith. Much can be done with the playing and the movements from area to area to heighten the impression of a seeking, the feeling of finding the way.

Set The set consists of four areas:

1. Down right a limbo area for the barker, with a fold-away stand of the sort used by street pitchmen.

2. Up right center a hospital bed and hospital screen.

3. Up left center a table with a checkered cloth and two chairs.

4. Down left a park bench and a tree.

Note that the table and chairs may be removed after they are used. This is not a must, but their presence will detract from DONALD's final scene should they be spilled on by the lights.

Props Several small matching bottles filled with clear liquid, one such filled with green liquid. A beer bottle and two beer glasses. A checkered tablecloth. A bunch of flowers.

Costumes For the barker a loud suit and bright vest, a straw hat (of the sennit or flat-top type) and cane. For ALEXANDRA college clothes and a hospital gown. For MARCELLA and DONALD casual clothes.

GENERAL PRODUCTION
NOTES

These brief notes on the plays in this volume are set down in the hope they will be of help to people who wish to stage the plays but are inexperienced in the theatre.

In these notes regular theatre practice has been followed with regard to stage directions. They are given from the actor's perspective, so that left is the *actor's* left, not the audience's. Down stage is *toward* the audience. The term "raked" means placed at an angle.

A prompt book will be found helpful. It may be prepared by placing between the pages of the book special insert sheets of tissue paper gummed along one edge. These pages can carry notes, directions, lighting diagrams and cues, etc.

Lighting will prove to be, perhaps, the most difficult single factor in live productions of these plays. With rare exceptions it is essential that only one stage area be lit at a time, and highly desirable that lights not spill over into other areas. For those who have not previously worked in the limbo technique, a handbook on lighting will prove helpful. All lighting cues should be rehearsed until they are letter perfect.